The flowering plants of South Africa vol. 3

By

I. B. Pole Evans

PUBLISHED BY: 2024 by BTB Publishing

ISBN : 978-1-63652-370-5

# THE FLOWERING PLANTS OF SOUTH AFRICA

VOL. 3

I. B. POLE EVANS

# CONTENTS

# PLATE 81.

*CLEMATOPSIS STANLEYI.*
*Transvaal. Tropical Africa.*

RANUNCULACEAE. *Tribe* CLEMATIDEAE.

CLEMATOPSIS, *Bojer MS. ex Hutchinson in Kew Bulletin*, 1920,
**Clematopsis Stanleyi**, *Hutchinson in Kew Bulletin, 1920,*
CLEMATIS STANLEYI, *Harv. in Harv. and Sond. Fl.*

In the *Botanical Magazine* (t. 7166) 1891, an excellent figure of this species was given with some critical notes by Sir Joseph Hooker on the taxonomic affinities of the species, and recently (Kew Bulletin, 1920) Mr. J. Hutchinson dealt more fully with the group represented by our plant. He has established Bojer's MS. name *Clematopsis*, under which he describes 15 species of which only *C. Stanleyi* occurs within our limits. The separation of *Clematopsis* from *Clematis* is based on the aestivation of the sepals and for a full account of these differences the reader is referred to Mr. Hutchinson's article. The chief interest in the genus is the fact that it forms a connecting link between the tribes *Anemoneae* and *Clematideae*, which were hitherto supposed to be sharply demarcated. It is confined to the ancient plateau of Africa and its continuation in Madagascar.

*Clematopsis Stanleyi* is a fairly common plant in parts of the Transvaal and has been recorded from the Pretoria, Witwatersrand, Waterberg, Middleburg Districts, and it extends into Rhodesia and Angola. In habit it is a small shrub 18 inches to 2 feet high and when in full bloom is a very pleasing object and well worth the attention of horticulturists. When in fruit the beauty of the plant is not entirely lost as the long white plumose styles stand out in sharp contrast to the surrounding vegetation.

The specimen figured here was collected by Miss S. Gower at Krugersdorp in February 1922.

DESCRIPTION:—A small shrub 45-60 cm. high. *Branches* ribbed, villous. *Leaves* opposite, 7-14 cm. long, bipinnate; the ultimate leaflets about 2 cm. long, pinnately lobed; lobes linear, acute, villous; petiole concave above, convex beneath, villous. *Peduncle* axillary and terminal, 3-8 cm. long, densely villous. *Sepals* 2 cm. long, 1·5 cm. broad, obovate, densely villous without and within. *Filaments* 8 mm. long, linear, pilose; anthers 4 mm. long. *Style* 1·2 cm. long, densely plumose. *Fruits* densely villous terminated by the persistent plumose style.

PLATE 81.—Fig. 1, stamens, front and side view; Fig. 2, a single carpel; Fig. 3, fruits with the persistent styles.

F.P.S.A., 1923.

K. A. LANSDELL DEL

# PLATE 82.

PROTEACEAE. *Tribe* PROTEEAE.

*MIMETES, Salisb.; Benth. et Hook. f. Gen. Plant.*

**Mimetes hottentotica**, *Phillips et Hutchinson*, sp. nov. insignis et affinitate *M. saxatili* Phill. foliis late ellipticis, capitulis paucis stigmate excavato differt.

*Rami* tomentosi et sparse villosi. *Folia* 4·5-7·5 cm. longa, 2·2-3·5 cm. lata, elliptica, apice tridentata, dense pubescentia pilis sericeis. *Capitula* sessilia, 7·5 cm. longa, 8-12-flora, apice ramorum conferta. *Involucri* bracteae 3-seriatae, 1·7-2 cm. longae, 3-6 mm. latae, lanceolato-ovatae, lineares, vel lineari-lanceolatae, obtusae vel subacutae, villosae, ciliatae. *Segmenta perianthii* 3·2 cm. longa, linearia, paullo lata, villosa; limbus 6 mm. longus, obovatus, subacuminatus, apice obtusus, villosus. *Antherae* 2·5 mm. longae, apice obtusae. *Squamae hypogynae* 3 mm. longae, lineares, apice subacutae. *Ovarium* 1 mm. longum, villosum; stylus 6·5 mm. longus, glaber; stigma 4 mm. longum, obovoideum, apice obtusum, excavatum.

SOUTH AFRICA: Caledon Division. Hottentot's Holland Mountains near Hangklip, *T. P. Stokoe in National Herbarium*, 1641.

Mr. T. P. Stokoe, to whom we are indebted for so many of the

4

interesting plants figured in earlier plates of this work, has again contributed two exquisite species of *Mimetes* which are both un-described. Unfortunately, it was not possible at the time to figure both plants, but we hope to publish a figure and description of the second species in our next volume. The genus, which is represented by nine species, falls into two well-defined groups, (*a*) those with an ovoid stigma (represented by *M. capitulata*, figured on Plate 58) and (*b*) those species with a linear stigma (represented by *M. palustris*, figured on Plate 36). Hitherto only two species of the first group were known, but these recent acquisitions from Mr. Stokoe increases this number to four.

The species figured in the accompanying plate was found on the Hottentot's Holland Mountains S.E. of Kogelberg and was growing on the banks of a steep, fairly moist slope. When fresh, it is a most beautiful object, certainly one of the most handsome species of the genus. The styles are bright red, white just below the stigma, and the stigma brownish-black. It is characterised by the regular excavations on the surface of the stigma which appear to be receptacles for the pollen grains.

Specimens are preserved in the National Herbarium, Pretoria (Herb. No. 1641).

DESCRIPTION:—*Branches* minutely tomentose but also sparsely covered with long lax hairs. *Leaves* 4·5-7·5 cm. long, 2·2-3·5 cm. broad, elliptic, with a blunt 3-toothed callous apex, densely adpressed-pubescent with silky hairs. *Heads* sessile, 7·5 cm. long including the styles, 8-12-flowered, solitary in the axils of the leaves at the ends of the branches. *Involucral-bracts* 3-seriate; the outer 1·7 cm. long, 6 mm. broad, lanceolate-ovate, obtuse, villous without, long-ciliate; inner 2 cm. long, 3 mm. broad, linear or linear-lanceolate, sub-acute, villous without, long-ciliate. *Recep-*

*tacle* villous. *Perianth* divided almost to the base; segments 3·2 cm. long, linear-filiform, slightly broadened at the base, villous; limb 6 mm. long, obovate, subacuminate, obtuse, villous. *Anthers* sessile, 2·5 mm. long, obtuse. *Hypogynous scales* 3 mm. long, linear subacute. *Ovary* about 1 mm. long, hairy at base; style 6·5 mm. long, cylindric, glabrous; stigma 4 mm. long, obovoid, obtuse, with several depressions on the sides.

PLATE 82.—Fig. 1, a single head; Fig. 2, bracts; Figs. 3, 4, a single flower; Fig. 5, perianth-segment enlarged; Fig. 6, stigma enlarged.

F.P.S.A., 1923.

K. A. LANSDELL DEL

# PLATE 83.

COMPOSITAE. *Tribe* SENECIONIDEAE.

*SENECIO, Linn.; Benth. et Hook. f. Gen. Plant.*

**Senecio Medley-Woodii**, *Hutchinson*, sp. nov. succulenta caule crasso, foliis carnosis dentatis lanato-pubescentibus, capitulis speciosis flavis distincta.

*Rami* succulenti, purpurei, juniores lanati, demum glabri. *Folia* sessilia, 3·5-5 cm. longa, 1·5-3 cm. lata, obovata, breviter apiculata, basi cuneata, superne undulato-dentata, primum lanata, demum plus minusve glabra. *Capitula* racemoso-corymbosa, 13-14-flora, 19 cm. longa; pedunculi ultimi 3-6 cm. longi, lanati. *Involucri bracteae* 1·2-1·5 cm. longae, 3-6 mm. latae, lanceolatae ad elliptico-ovatae, obtusae, marginibus membranaceis, extra lanato-tomentosae. *Receptaculum* planum, 8 mm. latum, foveolatum. *Flores radii* flavi; limbus 1·5 cm. longus, 5 mm. latus, oblongus, 6-8-nervus, apice minute tridentatus; ovarium glabrum. *Flores disci* brunneo-flavi; pappus 1 cm. longus; corollae tubus 1·2 cm. longus, glaber. *Achaenia* glabra.

This is one of the shrubby species of *Senecio* with succulent stems found in Natal. In cultivation it makes an ornamental shrub having very large yellow-rayed heads. The species was first collected by the late Dr. Medley Wood at Murchison in Natal in 1884

(*Wood* 3065), and was brought to him from Krantzkloof in August 1915. Dr. Wood had an illustration made for vol. vii of the "Natal Plants," but did not draw up a description, as specimens were sent to Kew for identification. The present illustration was made from a specimen which flowered in the garden of the Natal Herbarium. This species was the last which Dr. Medley Wood worked at the day before his death.

Specimens are preserved in the National Herbarium, Pretoria (Herb. No. 1604).

DESCRIPTION:—*Branches* succulent, woolly when young, at length becoming glabrous. *Leaves* sessile, 3·5-5 cm. long, 1·5-3 cm. broad above, obovate, shortly apiculate, cuneate at the base, with the margins more or less undulate and sometimes toothed in the upper half, woolly when young, at length becoming more or less glabrous. *Inflorescence* terminal, peduncled, 13-14-flowered, racemose-corymbose, 19cm. long; common peduncle 10 cm. long, woolly; ultimate peduncles 3-6cm. long, few-bracteate, woolly. *Bracts* 1·5-2cm. long, linear, obtuse, woolly. *Involucral-scales* 1·2-1·5cm. long, 3-6 mm. broad, lanceolate to elliptic-ovate, obtuse, with more or less membranous margins, woolly-tomentose without. *Receptacle* flat, 8mm. broad, honeycombed. *Ray-flowers* pale yellow. *Corolla-tube* 6mm. long, cylindric; limb 1·5cm. long, 5mm. broad, oblong, 6-8-nerved, minutely 3-toothed at the apex. *Pappus* 9mm. long; setae very minutely barbellate. *Ovary* 4mm. long, linear in outline, glabrous; style 8mm. long, cylindric, somewhat thickened at the base; lobes 2mm. long, linear obtuse. *Disc-flowers* brownish-yellow. *Pappus* 1cm. long, very minutely barbellate. *Corolla-tube* 1·2cm. long, gradually widening upwards, glabrous; lobes 1·5mm. long, ovate, obtuse. *Filaments* inserted at the constricted portions of the corolla-tube, 6mm. long, linear, slightly broadened below the anthers; anthers 4mm. long, with a short ovate appendage, blunt at the base. *Ovary* 4·5mm. long, linear in outline, glabrous; style 1·1cm. long, cylindric; lobes 2mm. long, flat on the inner face, convex on the back, truncate and shortly bristly at the apex.

---

PLATE 83.—Fig. 1, ray-flower; Fig. 2, disc-flower; Fig. 3, upper portion of style with lobes; Figs. 4, 5, involucral bracts; Fig. 6, fruit.

F.P.S.A., 1923.

S. GOWER DEL

# PLATE 84.

*PROTEA COMPACTA.*
*Cape Province.*

---

PROTEACEAE. Tribe PROTEEAE

*PROTEA, Linn.; Benth. et Hook. f. Gen. Plant.*
**Protea compacta**, *R. Br. in Trans. Linn. Soc. vol. x. 76; Fl.*

---

We have previously figured two species of *Protea* belonging to different sections of the genus. On Plate 22 will be found *P. abyssinica* (§ *Lasiocephalae*) with a large head not contracted into a scaly peduncle at the base, while on Plate 76 we figured *P. recondita* (§ *Leiocephalae*) with a smaller head and a scaly peduncle. Our present plant belongs to quite a separate section (*Ligulatae*), which is characterised by the inner involucral bracts being produced into a long claw with an oblong or oblanceolate limb. *Protea compacta* is a common plant in some parts of the Cape Province, especially in the Caledon Division, but is also found in parts of the Cape and Stellenbosch Divisions, and a single specimen, collected by Zeyher, has been recorded from the van Staden's Mountains. In its natural habitat it is a bush 4-6 ft. high with brilliant pink bracts partly surrounded by the uppermost leaves, and in many localities the flowering bush is one of the features of the landscape. Like many other species of *Protea* in the Cape Province, this species is visited by a large coleopterous beetle.

Our plant was collected by Dr. I. B. Pole Evans, C.M.G., at Hawston in the Caledon Division, where it is found growing on white sandy soil. The species has been established in cultivation at the National Botanic Gardens, Kirstenbosch, and is doing remarkably well there. Specimens are preserved in the National Herbarium, Pretoria (No. 2577).

DESCRIPTION:—*Branches* finely tomentellous, at length glabrous. *Leaves* 3¼-4½ in. long, ¾-1½ in. broad, strongly imbricate, ovate to ovate-lanceolate or elliptic-oblong, obtuse with a callous point, sub-cordate or rounded or slightly narrowed at the base, coriaceous, prominently veined, glabrous, with the margins shortly villous or at length glabrous. *Head* sessile, 4 in. long, about 2½ in. in diameter. *Involucral-bracts* 8-seriate; outer ovate, obtuse, villous-pubescent or more or less glabrescent, with a dense fringe of woolly hairs; inner more or less flesh-colour to carmine with an oblong limb and a linear claw, finely villous-tomentose, tips densely ciliate, exceeding the flowers. *Perianth-sheath* 2 in. long, dilated, 5-nerved and 3-keeled below, finely tomentose, glabrous at the base; lip over 1 in. long, 3-awned, lateral awns 3-4½ in. long, filiform, flexuous, tawny to purplish-tomentose; median awn 1 in. long, filiform. *Fertile stamens* 3, sub-sessile; filaments ¾ in. long, flattened; anthers linear, 4½ in. long; apical gland almost 1 in. long, lanceolate-oblong; barren stamen 4½ in. long, linear, eglandular. *Ovary* 1 in. long, oblong, densely covered with long light-golden hairs; style 2 in. long, finely grooved on the convex side, glabrous; stigma 2½ in. long, linear, obtuse, strongly keeled and bent at the junction with the style.

---

PLATE 84.—Fig. 1, longitudinal section of receptacle; Fig. 2, surface view of portion of receptacle; Fig. 3, an outermost bract; Fig. 4, inner bract; Fig. 5, a single flower; Fig. 6, ovary and base of style; Fig. 7, stigma and upper part of style.

F.P.S.A., 1923.

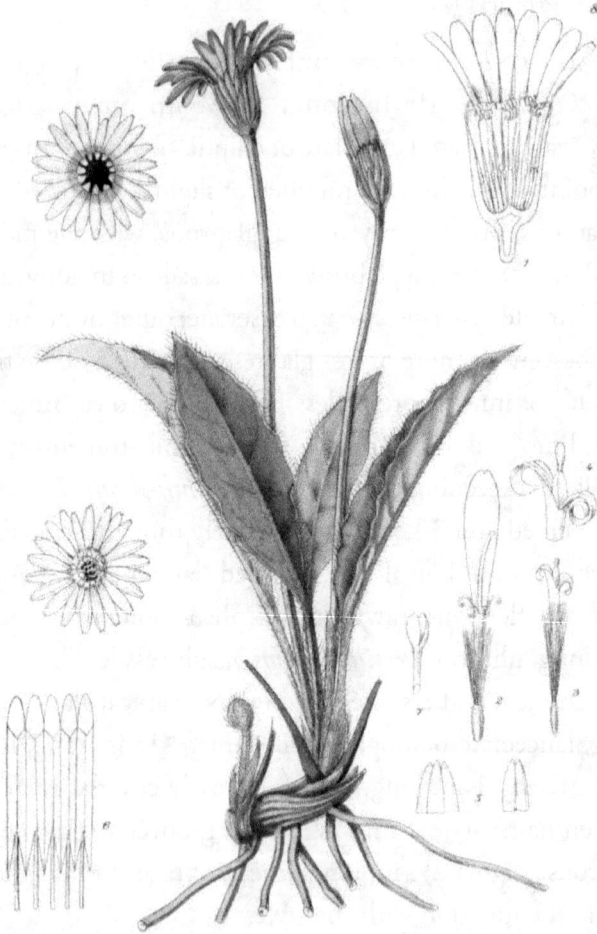

S. GOWER DEL.

# PLATE 85.

*GERBERA PLANTAGINEA.*
*Transvaal.*

---

COMPOSITAE. *Tribe* MUTISIEAE.

*GERBERA, Gronov.; Benth. et Hook. f. Gen. Plant.*
**Gerbera plantaginea**, *Harv. in Fl.*

---

In an earlier part, on Plate 64, we figured a Transvaal plant, *Gazania pygmaea*, and stated it to be one of the first species to flower on burnt veld. The plant illustrated here is usually contemporary with the above, and before any of the other veld plants show signs of growth numerous inflorescences of *Gerbera plantaginea* may be seen pushing through the hard surface of the soil. The underground rootstock is well adapted to withstand the long, dry winter months, and can store up sufficient moisture to commence growth before the first summer rains begin. The plant is usually found growing in small colonies, and the colour of the ray-florets varies from pure white to yellow and through various shades of pink to red. Like *Gazania pygmaea*, this species was found by Burke and Zeyher on the Magaliesberg about the year 1841, and Harvey, in the "Flora Capensis," based his description on their specimen. We are indebted to Mr. D. Fouche for the specimens which were collected near Meintjes Kopje, Pretoria. They are preserved in the National Herbarium, Pretoria (Herb. No. 2580).

DESCRIPTION:—An acaulescent plant with an underground rhizome with a woolly crown and thick cylindric roots. *Leaves* 4·5-13cm. long, 0·8-2·2cm. broad, lanceolate or oblong-lanceolate, subacute, narrowed into a petiole at the base, with the midrib and lateral veins distinct beneath, and with entire or sub-denticulate margins, pilose above and beneath. *Peduncle* 11-27cm. long, naked, densely tomentose, at length becoming sparsely tomentose. *Heads* solitary, 3-4cm. in diameter. *Involucral-bracts* in 3 rows, all tomentose; the outer 7 mm. long, 1·5 mm. broad at the base, tapering to an acute point; the inner 1 cm. long, 2 mm. broad, lanceolate, acuminate, acute. *Receptacle* slightly convex, honeycombed. *Ray-flowers* in two rows; the outer with a strap-shaped limb 1 cm. long, 2·5 mm. broad, about 6-nerved, minutely 2-3-toothed at the apex and with the lower lip represented by 4 linear appendages 1·5-2 mm. long, the two outer narrower than the two inner. *Pappus* 6 mm. long, longer than the tube. *Ovary* 3 mm. long, oblong, pilose; style 8 mm. long, cylindric; lobes 0·5 mm. long, glandular (lobes sometimes three); inner ray-flowers similar to the outer but limb 4·5 mm. long, 0·75 mm. broad. *Disc-flowers* hermaphrodite. *Corolla-tube* 4·5 mm. long, cylindric; lobes 3 mm. long, 0·5 mm. broad, linear, obtuse. *Anthers* 5 mm. long, linear, obtuse, long-tailed at the base. *Pappus* 6 mm. long. *Ovary* 3 mm. long, terete, almost glabrous; style 6 mm. long, cylindric; lobes 0·5 mm. long, ovate, obtuse.

---

PLATE 85.—Fig. 1, longitudinal section through head showing the convex receptacle; Fig. 2, a ray-floret; Fig. 3, a disc-floret; Fig. 4, upper portion of corolla of disc-floret; Fig. 5, apices of lips of disc-floret; Fig. 6, stamens; Fig. 7, upper portion of style of disc-floret showing the two lobes.

F.P.S.A., 1923.

# PLATE 86.

*ALOE* VARIEGATA.
*Cape Province.*

LILIACEAE. Tribe ALOINEAE.

*ALOE, Linn.; Benth. et Hook. f. Gen. Plant.*
**Aloe variegata**, *Linn. Sp. Pl.*

The *Aloe* here represented differs from any we have previously illustrated by having the leaves arranged in three ranks which may become spirally twisted. In the "Flora Capensis" this character is used to distinguish a sub-genus "Gonialoe" which contains only the species *A. variegata.* The species is one of the oldest and most common aloes in cultivation. A coloured illustration appeared in the *Botanical Magazine* (t. 513) in 1801, and it is recorded that a Mr. Fairchild had the species growing in England in 1720. For some reason the plant is not well represented in European herbaria, as even in 1897, when the genus was published in the "Flora Capensis," the precise localities in which the species occurs in South Africa remained doubtful. The traveller and botanist, Carl Thunberg, collected the plant about 1772, and according to Mr. N. E. Brown it is represented in the Thunberg herbarium by "two leaves with the variegation on them well preserved, and a single flower."

The species is easy of cultivation and is propagated by means of suckers which send up small plants. From the plant in cultivation at Pretoria, four offshoots have developed in one season.

We are enabled to figure this plant through the courtesy of Mrs. E. Rood, of Van Rhynsdorp, who forwarded us the living plant, which flowered at Pretoria in July 1922. Specimens are preserved in the National Herbarium, Pretoria (No. 2575).

DESCRIPTION:—An acaulescent plant. *Leaves* in three rows sometimes slightly spirally twisted, with irregular greenish-white bands on a dark green background; the lower leaves 8-10 cm. long, about 3·5 cm. broad, ovate, mucronate, almost flat above, keeled beneath, rough with small tubercles on the keel and margins; the inner leaves 14-23 cm. long, ovate-lanceolate, mucronate, concave on the inner face, keeled beneath, rough with small tubercles on the keel and margins. *Inflorescence* from the axil of one of the lower leaves; peduncle 40 cm. long, 9 mm. in diameter, terete, with about 8 barren bracts below the flowers which occupy the uppermost 11 cm. of the peduncle. *Flowers* at first erect, then horizontal, then pendulous when mature. *Bracts* 1·2 cm. long, 6 mm. broad, long-acuminate, acute, longer than the pedicels, white, with a greenish-brown keel. *Pedicels* 5 mm. long, terete, glabrous. *Perianth-tube* 4 cm. long, 9 mm. in diameter, tubular, slightly ventricose and oblique at the base; lobes 9 mm. long, 5 mm. broad, obovate. *Stamens* attached to the base of the perianth; filaments 4·5 cm. long, terete; anthers 2·5 mm. long, oblong. *Ovary* 6 mm. long, 3 mm. in diameter, ellipsoid; style 4 cm. long, terete; stigma minutely 3-lobed.

---

PLATE 86.—Fig. 1, bract; Fig. 2, bud; Fig. 3, mature flower; Fig. 4, upper part of perianth laid open; Fig. 5, stamen; Fig. 6, pistil; Fig. 7, cross-section of leaf. N.B.—In the coloured drawing the leaves are half natural size, but the inflorescence is natural size.

F.P.S.A., 1923.

S. GOWER DEL.

# PLATE 87.

*CERATOTHECA TRILOBA.*
*Bechuanaland, Cape Province, Natal, Transvaal.*

PEDALLACEAE. Tribe SESAMEAE.

*CERATOTHECA, Endl.; Benth. et Hook. f. Gen. Plant.*
**Ceratotheca triloba**, *E. Mey. ex Bernh. in Linnaea,*

The genus *Ceratotheca*, of which there are five species known, is confined to Africa, but the species figured in the accompanying plate is the only one recorded in South Africa. The genus is closely related to *Sesamum*, only differing by the capsule having two divergent horns or spines at the apex instead of being acute or beaked as in the latter genus. The species was first described in 1842 under the name *Sporledera triloba*, but, as pointed out in the *Botanical Magazine* under Tab. 6974, there is no justification for establishing a genus to include this species separate from *Ceratotheca*. The oldest record from South Africa appears to be specimens collected by Drège between the Umtata and St. John's River, but since then it has been found by numerous collectors. When fresh, the leaves have a very objectionable odour. The plant is very common during January on the hills at Wonderboom, near Pretoria. Our specimen was collected by Dr. R. Reitz. Specimens are preserved in the National Herbarium, Pretoria (No. 1605).

DESCRIPTION:—An herbaceous plant with erect stems, sometimes 6 ft. high, simple or branched. *Stems* obtusely 4-angled, glandular-pilose. *Leaves* opposite, sometimes alternate, petiolate; petioles 0·5-5 cm. long, grooved above, convex beneath, glandular-pilose; lamina 2-6·5 cm. long, ovate, more or less 3-lobed with the lobes crenate (the uppermost leaves not lobed), cordate at the base, palmately veined, with the veins prominent beneath, depressed above, glandular-pubescent. *Flowers* solitary, axillary, with often two abortive flowers in the same leaf-axil. *Pedicels* 5 mm. long, terete, glandular-pilose. *Calyx* divided almost to the base; the lobes erect, 0·8-1 cm. long, lanceolate, acuminate, sub-obtuse, glandular-pilose; the anterior lobe the smallest. *Corolla-tube* 3·5 cm. long, ventricose at the base, then slightly constricted and widening into a broad campanulate portion 1·4 cm. diameter, glandular-pilose; lobes 0·8 cm. long, about 1 cm. broad, transversely oblong, rounded above; the posterior lobe longer. *Stamens* of two different lengths, inserted above the ventricose portion of the corolla-tube; filaments 0·9-1·3 cm. long, glabrous; anthers 5 mm. long, linear. *Ovary* 6 mm. long, oblong in outline, densely villous, with 2 divergent horns at the apex; style 1·8 cm. long, terete, glabrous; stigmas recurved, papillose. *Fruit* 2 cm. long, oblong, with 2 divergent horns, glandular-pilose.

---

PLATE 87.—Fig. 1, portion of flowering branch; Fig. 2, corolla laid open; Fig. 3, pistil; Fig. 4, cross-section of ovary; Fig. 5, stigmas; Fig. 6, stamens and anther; Fig. 7, fruits; Fig. 8, fruit dehisced; Fig. 9, leaf; Figs. 10, 11, abortive flowers.

F.P.S.A., 1923.

S. GOWER DEL.

# PLATE 88.

*DICOMA ZEYHERI.*
*Transvaal. Zululand.*

COMPOSITAE. *Tribe* MUTISIEAE.

*DICOMA, Cass.; Benth. et Hook. f. Gen. Plant.*
**Dicoma Zeyheri**, *Cass. in Linn.*

The genus *Dicoma* comprises a small group of half-woody shrubs with acuminate usually pungent involucral-bracts. About twenty-five species are known, most of which are found in Tropical and South Africa, one extending into Western India. There is also a peculiar species, *D. cana*, in the island of Socotra. The tribe *Mutisieae*, to which *Dicoma* belongs, is but sparingly represented in Africa and has its head-quarters in South America.

Our present plant is common in parts of the Transvaal Highveld, and is found in flower from January to March. It has also been collected at Barberton by Mr. E. E. Galpin. Like so many of the shrubby plants occurring in the grass-veld, it has deep underground roots from which the stems arise, but, unlike the majority of them, is one of the last to flower.

The specimen from which this plate was prepared was collected by Miss S. Gower near the Botanical Laboratories, Pretoria. Specimens are preserved in the National Herbarium, Pretoria (No. 2581).

DESCRIPTION:—A somewhat woody undershrub about 30 cm. high with deep underground roots. *Stems* striate, cobwebby. *Leaves*

5·5-7 cm. long, 1-1·7 cm. broad, lanceolate, acute, or obtuse, sometimes subacuminate, slightly broadened and half-clasping at the base, usually entire, more rarely minutely and remotely toothed, glabrous above, cobwebby beneath. *Capitulum* shortly peduncled, about 5 cm. in diameter when expanded. *Involucral-bracts* in about 8 rows, the outermost strongly reflexed, the rest erect spreading, 1·5-2·5 cm. long, 4-9 mm. broad, ovate, acuminate, pungent, with membranous margins (except the outermost); the innermost bracts erect, closely enveloping the flowers, almost wholly membranous. *Involucre* 1·5 cm. in diameter, slightly convex, deeply honey-combed. *Flowers* all hermaphrodite. *Corolla-tube* 6 mm. long, cylindric for 5 mm. then suddenly campanulate, glabrous; lobes 4·5 mm. long, linear, gradually tapering upwards, obtuse, recurved in open flowers. *Stamens* inserted at the widened portion of the corolla-tube; filaments 1·5 mm. long, linear; anthers 7·5 mm. long, linear, lanceolate, acute at the apex, long-tailed at the base; tails hairy with ascending hairs. *Ovary* densely villous; style 1·5 cm. long, cylindric, glabrous; lobes 0·5 mm. long, ovate, obtuse, convex and hairy on outer side. *Pappus* 9 mm. long, dense and completely hiding the corolla-tube; setae long, plumose.

PLATE 88.—Fig. 1, longitudinal section of head; Fig. 2, surface view of part of receptacle; Fig. 3, involucral-bract; Fig. 4, an inner involucral-bract; Fig. 5, disc-floret before style appears; Fig. 6, disc-floret with style through the stamens; Fig. 7, disc-floret with pappus removed; Fig. 8, stamen; Fig. 9, apex of style; Fig. 10, a single pappus bristle; Fig. 11, portion of a leaf showing the minute teeth on the margin.

F.P.S.A., 1923.

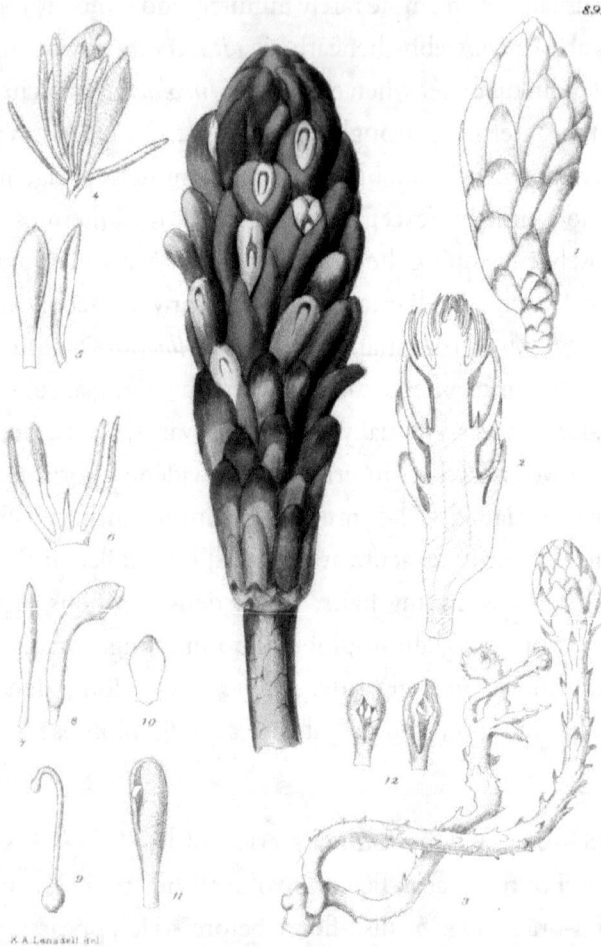

K A LANSDELL DEL

# PLATE 89.

SCROPHULARIACEAE. TRIBE GERARDIEAE.

*HYOBANCHE, Thunb.; Benth. et Hook. f. Gen. Plant.*

**Hyobanche Fulleri**, *Phillips*, sp. nov. *Stipes* succulentus. *Folia* 1·4 cm. longa, superne 6 mm. lata, spathulata, apice obtusa, externe glanduloso-villosa. *Inflorescentia* ad 13 cm. longa, 3 cm. lata. *Bracteae* 2·5 cm. longae, superne 6 mm. latae, spathulatae, externe glanduloso-pilosae, 3-nervosae; bracteolae 2, 2·5 cm. longae, 2 mm. latae, lineares, apice subacutae. *Pedicellus* 3 mm. longus, 3 mm. latus, carnosus. *Calyx* inaequalis; segmentum infimum 3 mm. longum, lineare; cetera 2·5 cm. longa, pilosa. *Corolla* leviter curvata, 3·5 cm. longa, 7 mm. lata, superne viscido-pilosa. *Filimenta* 2·4 cm. longa. *Ovarium* 4 mm. longum, globosum, glabrum; stylus 2·7 cm. longus, superne curvatus; stigma clavatum.

This new *Hyobanche* is the only recorded species for Natal. Bews ("Flora of Natal and Zululand") records *H. sanguinea* from Umzumbi, but we suspect it is the species here described. It was first collected by the late Dr. J. Medley Wood (Herb. Natal 11002) at Karridene Beach, and recently Mr. Claude Fuller of Pretoria forwarded living specimens from the same locality. Mr. Fuller was unable to determine the host on which the parasite grew. It differs from *H. sanguinea*, as from all the other known South

27

African species, in having the lowest calyx segment very much shorter than the others. The genus *Hyobanche* is very closely related to *Harveya*, a species (*Harveya squamosa*) of which is figured on Plate 67. Species of the two genera can easily be distinguished by an examination of the stamens. In *Hyobanche* the anthers are one-celled, while in *Harveya* the anthers are two-celled but only one cell contains pollen. Specimens are preserved in the National Herbarium, Pretoria (Herb. No. 1643).

DESCRIPTION:—A parasitic herb. *Stem* fleshy. *Leaves* adpressed, 1·4 cm. long, 6 mm. broad above, spathulate, obtuse, glandular-villous without. *Inflorescence* up to 13 cm. long, 3 cm. in diameter; axis fleshy. *Bracts* 2·5 cm. long, 0·6 cm. broad above, spathulate, densely glandular-pilose without, 3-nerved above; bracteoles 2, 2·5 cm. long, 2 mm. broad, linear, subacute, narrowing at the base. *Pedicels* 3 mm. long, 3 mm. in diameter, fleshy. *Calyx* unequal; the anterior segment 3 mm. long, linear; the lateral and posterior segments 2·5 cm. long, pilose without. *Corolla* slightly curved, 3·5 cm. long, 7 mm. in diameter, viscously pilose without in the upper half; mouth a longitudinal slit, about 1 cm. long, more or less opening out upwards by a recurving of the margins which indicates the presence of a hooded faintly two-lobed upper lip and a very obscure lower lip split to the base. *Filaments* 2·4 cm. long, attached near base of corolla-tube. *Ovary* 4 mm. long, 4 mm. in diameter, globose, glabrous; style 2·7 cm. long, terete, gradually thickening and sharply curved above, glabrous; stigma clavate.

PLATE 89.—Fig. 1, young inflorescence; Fig. 2, longitudinal section of inflorescence; Fig. 3, underground stem with young inflorescence; Fig. 4, flower, with bract and two bracteoles; Fig.

5, bract, front and side view; Fig. 6, calyx; Fig. 7, bracteole; Fig. 8, corolla; Fig. 9, gynæcium; Fig. 10, leaf; Fig. 11, upper portion of corolla, side view; Fig. 12, upper portion of corolla, front view.

F.P.S.A., 1923.

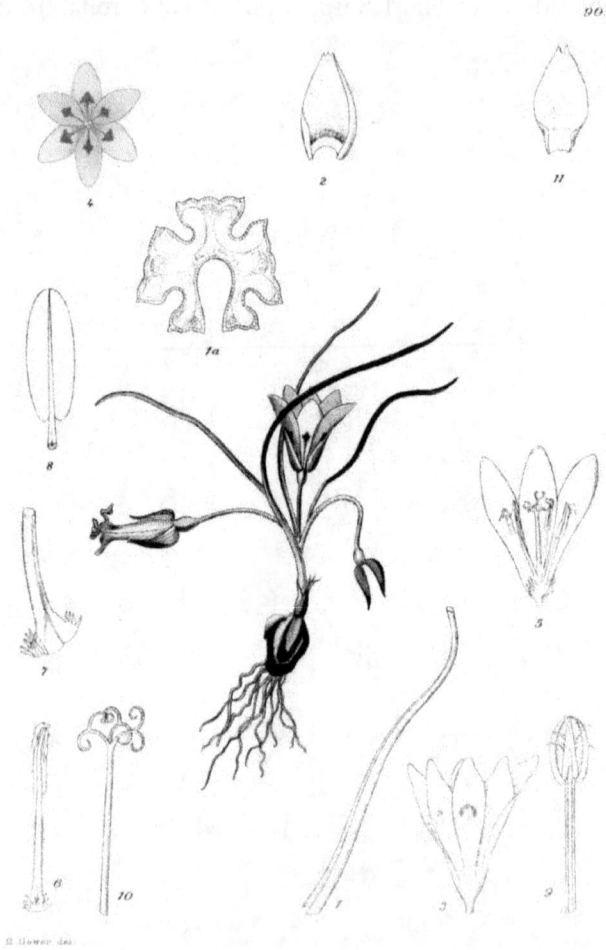

S. GOWER DEL.

# PLATE 90.

*ROMULEA AUSTINII.*
*Cape Province.*

IRIDACEAE. *Tribe* SISYRINCHIEAE.

*ROMULEA, Maratti; Benth. et Hook. f. Gen. Plant.*

**Romulea Austinii**, *Phillips*, sp. nov.; affinis *R. hirsutae*, Eck., sed floribus aurantiacis, bractea interior marginibus latis membranaceis differt.

*Cormi* 1·5 cm. longi, 1·2 cm. diametro, tunicis brunneis obtecti. *Folia* 3 vel 4, lineari-filiformia, acuta, 4-10 cm. longa, 0·75 mm. lata, profunde sulcata, basi vaginata. *Flores* 2-3-nati; pedicelli 1·2 cm. longi, subteretes, glabri, demum spiraliter curvati. *Valva* exterior elliptico-oblonga, herbacea, apice dentata, 9 mm. longa, 4 mm. lata, 9-nervia, marginibus angustis membranaceis, interior subaequalis, apice bifida, 5-6-nervia, marginibus latissime membranaceis. *Perianthii tubus* campanulatus, 5-6 mm. longus, lobis 1·5 cm. longis 0·7 cm. latis obovatis obtusis interioribus aurantiacis exterioribus purpureo notatis. *Filamenta* 9 mm. longa, basi explanata et pilosa, medio dorso pilosa; antherae 4 mm. longae, 2 mm. latae, ellipsoideae, primum leviter connatae. *Ovarium* subglobosum; stylus 1 cm. longus, teres, glaber, ramis 3·5 mm. longis bifidis.

SOUTH AFRICA: Matjesfontein, *A. J. Austin.*

We are indebted to Mr. A. J. Austin for this charming little species of *Romulea*, which is apparently undescribed. It was gathered at Matjesfontein. The same species was collected a few years ago by Schlechter (No. 8847) at Matjes River at an altitude of 2500 feet, and distributed by him as *Romulea hirsuta*, Eckl., var. *aurantiaca*. Although resembling *R. hirsuta* in general appearance, it is easily distinguished by the colour of the flowers and especially by the very broadly membranous margins of the inner spathe valve. The flowers close up at night.

Our knowledge of the genus *Romulea* in South Africa is still very meagre, and much field-work is necessary in order to understand the range and variability of the species.

DESCRIPTION:—*Corms* 1·5 cm. long, 1·2 cm. in diameter with brown tunics. *Leaves* 3-4 to a corm, 4-10 cm. long, 0·75 mm. broad, with five deep and narrow grooves, acute, somewhat sheathing at the base and forming a distinct neck, minutely ciliate. *Flowers* 2-3 to a spathe. *Pedicels* 1·2 cm. long, subterete, glabrous, becoming spirally coiled in old flowers. *Outer spathe valve* 9 mm. long, 4 mm. broad, elliptic-oblong, toothed at the apex, 9-nerved, with membranous margins; inner spathe valve about same size as outer, deeply bifid at the apex, 5-6-nerved with very broad membranous margins. *Perianth-tube* 5-6 mm. long, campanulate; lobes 1·5 cm. long, 0·7 cm. broad, obovate, obtuse, reflexed in the open flower, yellow in colour with a spade-like purple mark on the three outer and smaller purple marks on the three inner. *Filaments* 9 mm. long, convex on the back, grooved on the front face, broadened and pilose at the base, pilose on back about the middle; anthers 4 mm. long, 2 mm. broad, elliptic, in flowers which have just opened the anthers are somewhat joined and the stigmas appear between the anthers. Ovary subglobose;

style 1 cm. long, terete, glabrous; lobes 3·5 mm. long, each subdivided into 2 lobes 2 mm. long.

---

PLATE 90.—Fig. 1, leaf; Fig. 1*a*, section of leaf; Fig. 2, spathe valve; Fig. 3, perianth from outside; Fig. 4, same from above; Fig. 5, section of flower; Fig. 6, stamen; Fig. 7, base of filament; Fig. 8, anther (front); Fig. 9, anther (back); Fig. 10, style; Fig. 11, inner valve.

F.P.S.A., 1923.

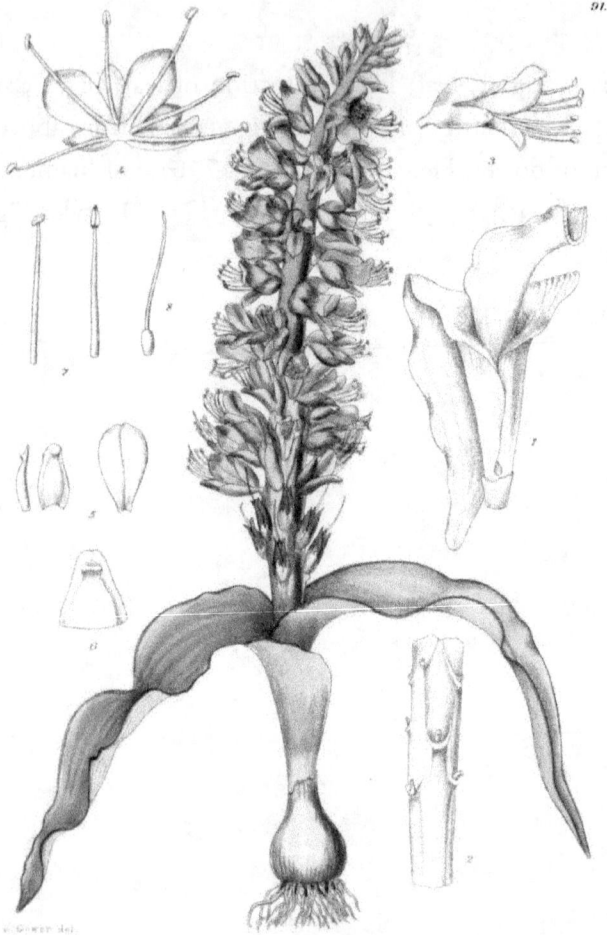

S. GOWER DEL.

# PLATE 91.

*LACHENALIA* ROODEAE.
Cape Province.

LILIACEAE. Tribe SCILLEAE.

*LACHENALIA, Jacq.; Benth. et Hook.*
**Lachenalia Roodeae,** *Phillips,* sp. nov.

*Bulbus* 2·5 cm. longus, 1·8 cm. latus. *Folia* 2, 7-14 cm. longa, basi 2-4 cm. lata, ovato-lanceolata, apice obtusa, aliquando mucronata, glabra. *Pedunculus* 2-3·5 cm. longus, c. 7 cm. latus. *Inflorescentia* spicata, 9-14 cm. longa. *Bracteae* c. 1 mm. longae, ovatae, apice obtusae. *Pedicellus* c. 1 mm. longus. *Flos* 1-1·2 cm. longus, campanulatus, basi obliquus; lobi exteriores 8 mm. longi, 4·75 mm. lati, oblongo-ovati, apice obtusi; lobi interiores 1 cm. longi, 4·5 mm. lati, oblongo-obovati, apice rotundi. *Stamina* exserta; filamenta 1·2 cm. longa; antherae 1·5 mm. longae, oblongae. *Ovarium* 3·5 mm. longum, 2·5 mm. latum, trigonum; stylus 1·1 cm. longus, teres; stigma minute 3-lobatum.

Van Rhynsdorp District: Van Rhynsdorp, *Mrs. E. Rood* in *National Herbarium Pretoria*, 1461.

This extremely fine species of *Lachenalia* was sent to the Division of Botany by Mrs. E. Rood of Van Rhynsdorp, who states that the plant is quite common there. It belongs to an endemic South African genus of about fifty species, and surpasses any other species known to us in the rich colouring of the flowers. It flowers during

August and September, and should make a welcome addition to the bulb garden as one of the earlier flowering species. There has been some doubt about the identity of this plant, and we were inclined to regard it as *L. carnosa*, Baker, which was collected by Drège in Little Namaqualand. Mr. N. E. Brown, of Kew, very kindly examined the plate, and is of the opinion that it is not this species, and that nothing like it is in the Kew Herbarium. It, however, is very near *L. carnosa*, Baker, but may be distinguished from this species in the inner perianth segments being longer than the outer and in the far exserted stamens. This latter character is not constant, as we find after examining a large series of specimens that the length to which the stamens are exserted from the perianth depends on the age of the flower. The stamens are in more or less two unilateral rows, the lower three ripening before the upper three.

DESCRIPTION:—*Bulb* 2·5 cm. long, 1·8 cm. in diameter, ovoid, covered with black membranous tunics with many fibrous roots from the base. *Leaves* 2, erect-spreading, 7-14 cm. long, 2-4 cm. broad in the widest part; the outer leaf always larger than the inner leaf, ovate-lanceolate, obtuse, sometimes mucronate, narrowed and clasping at the base, with reddish margins, glabrous. *Peduncle* 2-3·5 cm. long, about 7 mm. in diameter, partially hidden by the clasping leaf bases. *Inflorescence* a dense many-flowered spike, 9-14 cm. long; axis fleshy, up to 8 cm. in diameter at the base, narrowing upwards, with a number of facets, each facet bearing a flower at the base. *Bracts* about 1 mm. long, ovate, obtuse, forming a small pocket from which the flower arises. *Flowers* subsessile; pedicels about 1 mm. long. *Perianth* purplish, 1-1·2 cm. long, campanulate, oblique at the base; tube about 3 mm. long, about 5 mm. in diameter above; lobes of outer segments 8 mm. long, 4·75 mm. broad, oblong-ovate, obtuse, rostrate on the outer surface just beneath the apex; lobes of the inner segments 1 cm. long,

4·5 mm. broad above, oblong-obovate, rounded above. *Stamens* exserted, attached to base of the perianth segments; filaments 1·2 cm. long, terete; anthers 1·5 mm. long, oblong. *Ovary* 3·5 mm. long, 2·5 mm. in diameter, oblong in outline, trigonous; style 1·1 cm. long, terete, stigma very faintly 3-lobed.

PLATE 91.—Fig. 1, base of leaves; Fig. 2, axis of inflorescence showing the small cups in which the flowers are situated; Fig. 3, a single flower; Fig. 4, perianth laid open; Fig. 5, apices of outer perianth segments; Fig. 6, apex of an inner perianth segment. Fig. 7, stamens; Fig. 8, pistil.

F.P.S.A., 1923.

S. GOWER DEL.

# PLATE 92.

*BRUNIA STOKOEI.*
*Cape Province.*

---

BRUNIACEAE.

*BRUNIA, Linn.; Benth. et Hook. f. Gen. Plant.*
**Brunia Stokoei**, *Phillips in Kew Bulletin, 1923, ined.*

---

This is the first occasion upon which we have had an opportunity of figuring a member of the Natural Order *Bruniaceae*, which is one of the endemic South African families. The *Bruniaceae* comprise about fifty species, all confined to the south-western portion of the Cape Province. The genera *Brunia* and *Berzelia* often form a conspicuous feature in the landscape in some areas, the spherical heads of white flowers making the bushes noticeable amongst the surrounding vegetation.

The species figured here was collected in 1922 by Mr. T. P. Stokoe on the Hottentot Hollands Mountains near Hang Klip, and forwarded by him to the Division of Botany, Pretoria. Near the same locality Mr. Stokoe discovered another species of *Brunia*, which is undescribed. We do not know of either of these species having been previously collected, and the fact that undescribed and rare plants have recently been found on such a well-known mountain range as the Hottentot Hollands, proves that there must be a large area, within easy reach of Cape Town, which has not yet been thoroughly botanically explored.

DESCRIPTION:—*Branches* glabrous. *Leaves* spreading 7-8 mm.

long, 1 mm. broad, trigonous, almost flat above with a raised mid-rib, keeled beneath, obtuse, tipped with a small black globose mucro, the angles of the leaves when viewed by transmitted light are pellucid, glabrous. *Inflorescence* a stalked globose head arranged in groups up the branches. *Peduncles* 2-3 cm. long, 5-7 mm. in diameter, surrounded by adpressed imbricated bracts 3 mm. long, 1 mm. broad, lanceolate, obtuse, keeled below, glabrous. *Axis* of inflorescence 1·2-1·5 cm. long, 7-9 mm. in diameter, more or less ovate in longitudinal section. *Floral-bracts* 7 mm. long, obovate-spathulate, subacuminate, tipped with a black mucro, bent almost at right angles above, densely villous on back in the middle third. *Calyx* of 4 sepals, 4·5 mm. long; 3 sepals narrow-linear, the fourth oblanceolate, all densely villous without. *Petals* 5·5 mm. long, ·75 mm. broad, linear, with one large middle lobe and two small or almost obsolete side lobes. *Filaments* 5 mm. long, terete; anthers 1·25 mm. long, linear. *Ovary* 2 mm. long, 1 mm. in diameter, ellipsoid, densely villous above, 2-celled, with a pendulous ovule in each cell; styles two, 4 mm. long, terete, free from the base; stigma simple (in some flowers examined there was only a single style). *Immature fruit* 3·5 mm. long, 1·5 mm. in diameter, ellipsoid (National Herb. Pretoria 1668).

---

PLATE 92.—Fig. 1, longitudinal section through head showing axis of the inflorescence; Fig. 2, floral bract; Fig. 3, a single flower; Fig. 4, a stamen; Fig. 5, longitudinal section of ovary showing the two cells and pendulous ovules.

F.P.S.A., 1923.

*93.*

K. A. LANSDELL DEL.

# PLATE 93.

*HOODIA BAINII.*
*Cape Province.*

ASCLEPIADACEAE. TRIBE STAPELIEAE.

*HOODIA, Sweet.; Benth. et Hook. f. Gen. Plant.*
**Hoodia Bainii**, *Dyer in Bot. Mag. t. 6348; Fl.*

This plant, although previously figured in botanical publications, has been thought worthy of another illustration, especially as the former figures are not generally available to cultivators of South African succulents.

The first species of this interesting genus was brought to the notice of botanists in 1874 by Sir Henry Barkly, who sent specimens to Kew, where it flowered the following year. Since then other species have come to light, and we now know of seven species of the genus occurring in the desert regions of the Cape Province and Namaqualand.

The specimen figured was collected by Mrs. D. van der Bijl, Kruidfontein, Fraserburg District, in 1921, and sent to the Division of Botany, where it flowered in September 1922. The plant sends up numerous stems 9-12 inches high, and on these flowers profusely. The flowers are martius yellow (Ridgway Colour Standards) in colour, with a dark corona standing out in sharp relief in the middle of the saucer-shaped corolla. Like many other members of this group of plants, the flowers have a disagreeable odour.

DESCRIPTION:—Plant 6-8 in. high in the specimens seen (12-15 in. according to Barkly), bushily branched; branches 1-1½ in. thick, with 12-15 tuberculate angles, glabrous, green, somewhat glaucous; tubercles tipped with a slender pale brown spine 3½-5 in. long; flowers 1-2 together, glabrous in all parts; pedicels ¼-½ in. long; sepals 2-2½ in. long, ovate-lanceolate, acuminate; corolla in bud hemispheric at the basal part, 5-winged above, truncate, with a short central point, when expanded 2½-3 in. in diameter, cup-shaped, about 1 in. deep, subtruncate at the margin with 5 subulate or awn-like points 1½-3 in. long, glabrous, smooth, not papillate on the central part, light yellow or pale buff, sometimes tinged with pinkish or very pale purple; tube obsolete, represented by a slight depression from which the blackish corona is exserted or its margins resting upon the rim, when dried contained in a very small cup; outer corona 1¾-2 in. in diameter, cupular, 5-lobed; lobes ¼-⅓ in. long, nearly 1 in. broad, emarginate; inner corona-lobes ⅔ in. long, oblong, obtuse, closely incumbent upon the backs of the anthers and not exceeding them, dorsally connected to the inflexed sinuses of the outer corona; follicles 4-5 in. long, 4-5 in. thick, terete-fusiform, tapering to a beak, glabrous, smooth; seeds 3-3½ in. long, 1½ in. broad, ovate, flat, with a slightly thickened margin, glabrous, smooth, light brown. *Flora Capensis* (National Herb. Pretoria 2592).

———

PLATE 93.—Fig. 1, bud; Fig. 2, transverse section of stem; Fig. 3, corona; Fig. 4, pollinia.

F.P.S.A., 1923.

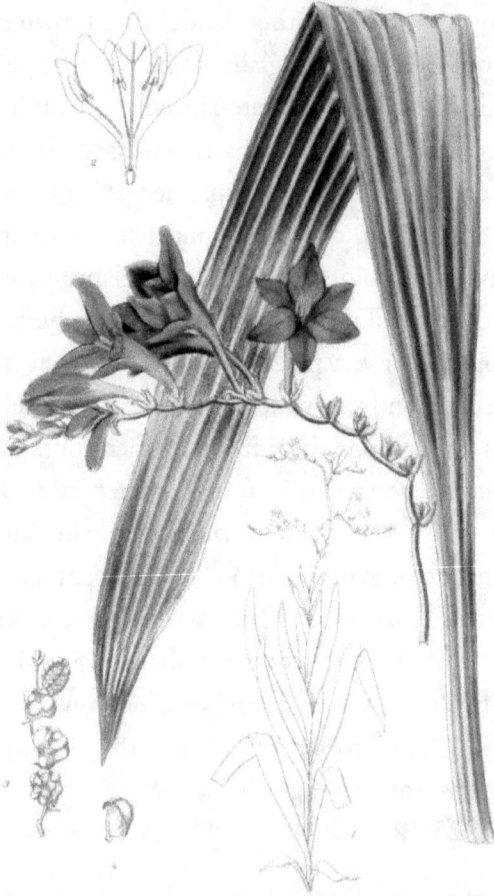

M. PAGE DEL.

# PLATE 94.

*TRITONIA MATHEWSIANA.*
*Transvaal.*

---

IRIDACEAE. *Tribe* IXIEAE.

*TRITONIA, Ker.; Benth. et Hook. f. Gen. Plant.*
**Tritonia Mathewsiana**, *L. Bolus in Annals Bolus Herb.*

---

This species, which belongs to one of the large South African gen-era of the iris family, differs from all genera of *Iridaceae* hitherto figured in this publication in having small brown spathe valves. The genus is represented in South Africa by over thirty species, mostly confined to the coastal region of the Cape Province, but with a few in Namaqualand, Natal, and the Transvaal. *Tritonia lineata* is the most widely distributed species of the genus, oc-curring in the Mossel Bay, Bathurst, Albany, Stockenstroom, and Somerset East Divisions, and extending into East Griqualand, Basutoland, and Natal.

The species here figured is a new record for the Transvaal, and was found by Mrs. H. M. Wood at Graskop, Pilgrim's Rest. Plants were sent to the National Botanic Gardens, Kirstenbosch, and flowered there during February of the years 1918-1921 (National Botanic Gardens, No. 542/16). An illustration was made from these specimens and kindly lent to us by the Curator of the Bolus Herbarium for reproduction.

DESCRIPTION:—An erect glabrous plant 1·5 mm. or more high. *Leaves* ascending or almost erect, 35 cm. long, 4 cm. broad, ensiform, with about 13 primary nerves; radical leaves about 4; cauline leaves about 10. *Peduncle* up to 15 cm. long clasped by the uppermost leaf which is reduced to 6 cm. long. *Inflorescence* racemose with the branches divaricate and the flowering axis flexuose, moderately dense with the flowers secund, at length perpendicular to the axis. *Bracts* 3-5 mm. long, oblong, acute, the younger herbaceous; bracteoles almost joined to their apices, acute, equalling the bracts. *Perianth* 3-3·5 cm. long; tube 1·8 cm. long, 1·5 mm. in diameter at the base, 5 mm. in diameter above, infundibuliform; segments at length spreading, ovate-oblong, obtuse; the outer 1·3 cm. long, 5 mm. broad; the inner 1·5 cm. long, 6 mm. broad; the uppermost 1·7 cm. long, 7 mm. broad. *Stamens* more or less curved; filaments 1·3 cm. long; anthers 5-7 mm. long. *Style* 2·3 cm. long; branches 5 mm. long. *Capsule* 8 mm. long, subglobose, obtusely 3-angled. *Seeds* many, 4 mm. long, subtriangular.

PLATE 94.—Fig. 1, whole plant (reduced); Fig. 2, flower laid open; Fig. 3, fruit; Fig. 4, seed × 2.

F.P.S.A., 1923.

95

K. A. LANSDELL DEL.

# PLATE 95.

*LEUCOSPERMUM* CORDATUM.
*Cape Province.*

---

PROTEACEAE. *Tribe* PROTEEAE.

*LEUCOSPERMUM, R. Br.; Benth. et Hook. f. Gen. Plant.*
**Leucospermum cordatum**, *Phillips in Kew Bulletin, 1923, ined.*

---

Although the South African *Proteaceae* are usually conspicuous plants and have been recently monographed in the *Flora Capensis*, undescribed species continue to be discovered. This is the case with the plant here figured, which was collected in November 1922 by Mr. T. P. Stokoe near Kogel Bai, on the Hottentots Holland Mountains at an altitude of 2500 ft.

Mr. Stokoe describes it as a plant of straggling growth among loose stones and grass. We have previously figured a species of this genus (Plate 74), and readers are referred to the description there for the principal differences between the genera *Protea* and *Leucospermum*.

The decumbent habit of this species is also found in *Leucospermum hypophyllum*, but is not common in the family.

Our plate was prepared from fresh plants forwarded by Mr. Stokoe.

DESCRIPTION:—A decumbent plant with long trailing branches. *Branches* scantily pilose with long hairs. *Leaves* more or less horizontal or slightly reflexed, 3-5 cm. long, 1·8-2·2 cm. broad at the base, ovate, obtuse with a blunt callus, cordate at the base, pilose and shortly tomentose especially near the base, at length becoming glabrous. *Heads* solitary, very rarely 3-nate at the ends of the branches, 3-4 cm. in diameter, semiglobose. *Peduncle* 2 cm. long, covered with numerous barren bracts, tomentose. *Bracts* 5 mm. long, 3 mm. broad, at the base, ovate, obtuse, sometimes reflexed, pilose outside, glabrous within, ciliate. *Receptacle* 7 mm. long, 5 mm. in diameter at the base, conical. *Floral-bracts* 1 cm. long, obovate, shortly awned, attenuate at the base, densely villous outside, glabrous within, ciliate. *Perianth-tube* 5 mm. long, tubular; lobes 9 mm. long, linear, long pilose; limb 3 mm. long, elliptic, subacuminate, sub-obtuse, pilose without. *Anthers* 2 mm. long, linear. *Ovary* 2·5 mm. long, ellipsoid, glabrous; style 1·7 cm. long, terete, glabrous; stigma 1·7 mm. long, conical, shortly subacuminate, swollen at the junction with the style (National Herb. Pretoria 2607).

PLATE 95.—Fig. 1, flower; Fig. 2, flower showing perianth lobes; Fig. 3, floral bract; Fig. 4, style and stigma; Fig. 5, longitudinal section of receptacle.

F.P.S.A., 1923.

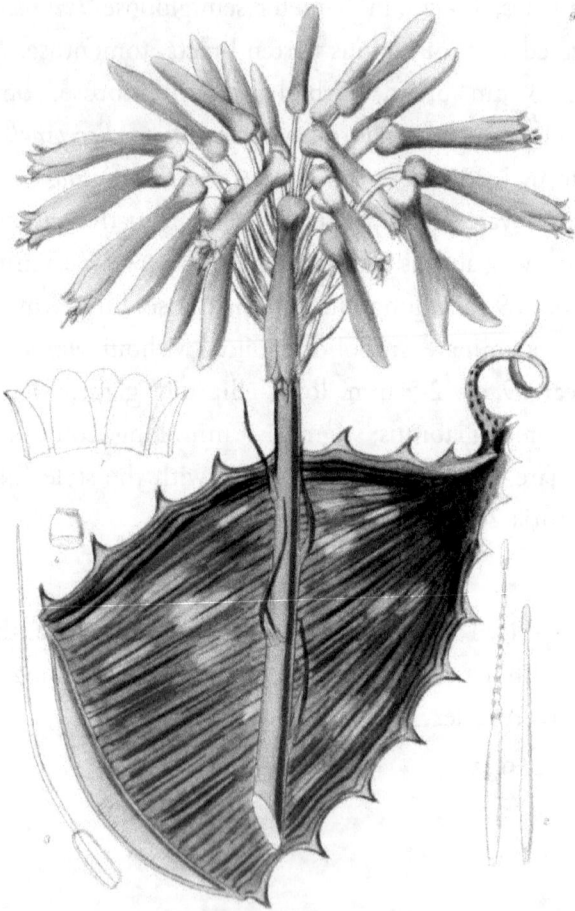

# PLATE 96.

*ALOE SAPONARIA.*
Cape Province, Natal, Transvaal.

LILIACEAE. *Tribe* ALOINEAE.

*ALOE, Linn.; Benth. et Hook. f. Gen. Plant.*
**Aloe saponaria**, *Haw. Syn. 83; Fl.*

This Aloe, known as the common soap-aloe, was introduced into cultivation in Europe early in the eighteenth century, and it still retains its popularity. Three colour varieties are known: one with salmon-coloured flowers, one with red flowers, and one with pale lemon-yellow flowers. The inflorescence in all these varieties may be either simple or branched. The plants are common on the south and east coasts of South Africa.

The buds just before the flowers open are between 3 and 4 cm. long, and in about four days are completely open, and then a little over 4 cm. long. The stamens do not all ripen at the same time; two or three project and shed their pollen, being followed after a short interval by the remainder. While the stamens are dehiscing the style remains within the perianth and lengthens only after the pollen has been shed. It then projects beyond the perianth, which now begins to wither and close tightly round the style. While this is taking place the filaments contract by twisting and are drawn back into the perianth. The inclusion of the style during the dehiscence of the anthers and its subsequent projection ensures cross-pollination.

Our plate was prepared from specimens growing in the Aloe collection at the Division of Botany, Pretoria.

DESCRIPTION:—An acaulescent plant or with a short stem with a rosette of leaves. *Leaves* up to 20 cm. long, about 8 cm. broad, dark green with dark longitudinal marking on the upper surface, lighter green and faintly spotted beneath, acuminate, usually brown and withered at the tip, with spines on the margins; spines 8 mm. long, about 1·5 cm. apart and more or less at right angles to the leaf. *Inflorescence* ·3–·5 m. high, simple or branched. *Peduncle* terete with a few dry membranous acuminate bracts. Flowers in a contracted raceme. *Floral bracts* 1·5-2·5 cm. long, long-acuminate from an ovate-lanceolate base. *Pedicels* 2·5-4 cm. long, terete. *Perianth-tube* 3·3 cm. long, 9 mm. in diameter above, gradually narrowing below and dilated into a globose base; segments 1 cm. long, ·5 cm. broad, oblong, obtuse, slightly reflexed in the mature flower. *Filaments* in buds 2·4 cm. long, linear, in mature flowers lengthening to 3·5 cm. and becoming corrugated in the upper half. *Ovary* 8 mm. long, cylindric; style 2·5 cm. long, cylindric, lengthening in older flowers to 3·8 cm.; stigma simple (National Herb. Pretoria 2593).

PLATE 96.—Fig. 1, perianth-lobes; Fig. 2, stamens; Fig. 3, pistil; Fig. 4, tip of style, much enlarged.

F.P.S.A., 1923.

M. PAGE DEL.

# PLATE 97.

*SYNNOTIA* METELERKAMPIAE.
*Cape Province.*

---

IRIDACEAE. *Tribe* IXIEAE.

*SYNNOTIA, Sweet.; Benth. et Hook. f. Gen. Plant.*
**Synnotia Metelerkampiae**, *L. Bolus in Annals Bolus Herb.*

---

The genus *Synnotia* is one of the endemic genera of the family *Iridaceae*, and has hitherto only been represented by two species. The species here figured is a new record for the genus in South Africa. On Plate 60 we figured a species of *Sparaxis*, and a comparison of that plate with the present one will show that the two genera *Sparaxis* and *Synnotia* are nearly related: the rootstock, inflorescence, and spathe valves are the same in both, but the former has regular flowers, while in the latter genus the flowers are irregular.

The species is found near Eendekuil in the Clanwilliam Division, and the original description was prepared from specimens flowering in the garden of Mrs. F. Metelerkamp. We are indebted to the Curator of the Bolus Herbarium for lending us the illustration from which the accompanying plate was prepared.

DESCRIPTION:—A glabrous herb, 16-25 cm. high. *Corm* 1·6 cm. long, 1·2 cm. in diameter, ovoid, with rigid tunics prominently nerved and with the nerves reticulated. *Stem* erect. *Leaves* 6-7 to each stem, 5-8 cm. long, 1-1·2 cm. broad, equitant, adscending, linear, obtuse, apiculate or acute, with inconspicuous nerves. *Inflorescence* racemose, laxly 9-12-flowered, with the flowers almost erect. *Bracts* clasping, about 2 cm. long, ovate; bracteoles united beyond the middle, setaceous-acuminate, almost equalling the bracts. *Perianth-tube* 4-4·5 cm. long, 1-2 mm. in diameter, oblique and expanding to 7 mm. in diameter above; segments unequal; the lower smaller than the upper; the outer segments 1·2 cm. long, 4-6 mm. broad, ovate-oblong, subacute; the inner segments subclawed, obtuse, and with obscurely undulate margins; the uppermost 1·4 cm. long, 8 mm. broad, ovate; the lower 5 mm. broad. *Filaments* 1·2 cm. long; anthers 3-5 mm. long, with purple pollen. *Style* 4·6 cm. long with spathulate branches 3 mm. long. *Capsule* 1·5 cm. long. *Seeds* many, 2 mm. in diameter, subglobose (Bolus Herb. Cape Town 16039).

---

PLATE 97.—Fig. 1, flower laid open; Fig. 2, capsule; Fig. 3, seed × 4; Fig. 4, corm.

F.P.S.A., 1923.

S. GOWER DEL.

# PLATE 98.

*CHRYSOPHYLLUM MAGALISMONTANUM.*
*Transvaal.*

---

SAPOTACEAE.

*CHRYSOPHYLLUM, Linn.; Benth. et Hook. f. Gen. Plant.*
**Chrysophyllum magalismontanum**, *Sond. in Linnaea,*

---

The genus *Chrysophyllum* is a small genus in South Africa, having only three representatives, two in Natal and one in the Transvaal. The species figured here is the common one in the Transvaal, being found all along the rocky outcrops of the Magaliesberg range and known as "stam vrucht," because the fruits are borne on the old stems. The fruits, which are oval in shape, are somewhat larger than a cherry, and are used to make preserve. The plants flower in October and ripe fruits are formed in January. A milky juice characteristic of all the species in the *Sapotaceae* is present in the plant. A member of the order, *Mimusops balata*, Crueg, native of Guiana, yields a guttapercha (balata).

The specimens from which our illustration was made were gathered at Eloff's Cutting near Pretoria by Mr. D. J. Fouche.

DESCRIPTION:—A bush. *Youngest* branchlets rufo-tomentose, at length becoming pubescent. *Leaves* petioled; blades 3-9 cm. long, 1·6-4·4 cm. broad, oblong-obovate or oblong, retuse at the apex, slightly narrowed at the base, dark green above, rufo-to-mentose beneath on young leaves, becoming greyish tomentose on the older leaves; petiole 1 cm. long, pubescent. *Flowers* arising on the old wood. *Pedicels* 2 mm. long, rufo-tomentose. *Sepals* unequal 2·5-3 mm. long, 2-3·5 mm. broad, ovate, obtuse; the 3 outer longer than the 2 inner and densely rufo-tomentose. *Corolla-tube* 1 mm. long; lobes 2·5 mm. long, ovate, obtuse. *Filaments* 1·5-2 mm. long, terete, glabrous; anthers 1 mm. long, oblong in outline. *Ovary* 2 mm. in diameter, villous, gradually passing into the 1·5 mm. long style; stigma terminal, simple. *Fruit* 2·5 cm. long, 1·7 cm. in diameter, ellipsoid, dark-red when ripe (National Herb. Pretoria 2636).

---

PLATE 98.—Fig. 1, flower; Fig. 2, portion of corolla and stamens; Fig. 3, stamen; Fig. 4, pistil; Fig. 5, seed.

F.P.S.A., 1923.

*92.*

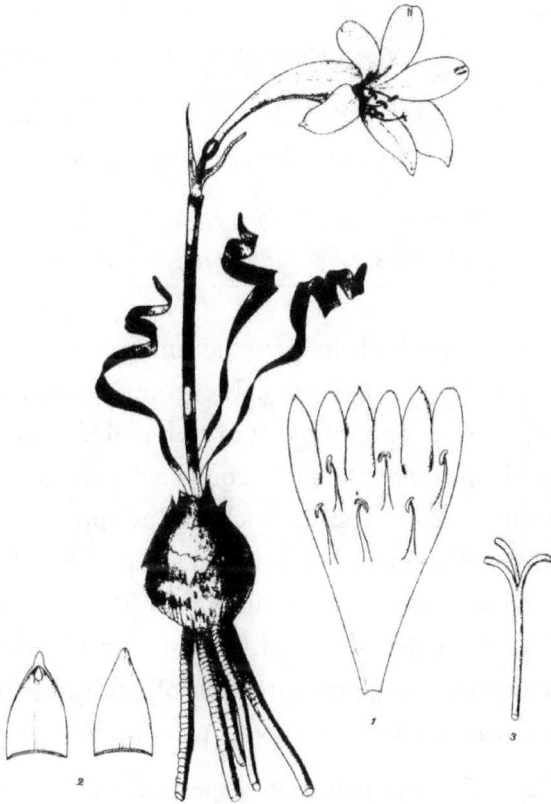

K A Lansdell del.

K A Lansdell del.

# PLATE 99.

*CYRTANTHUS HELICTUS.*
*Cape Province.*

---

AMARYLLIDACEAE. TRIBE AMARYLLEAE.

*CYRTANTHUS, Ait.; Benth. et Hook. f. Gen. Plant.*
**Cyrtanthus helictus**, *Lehm. Delect. Sem. Hort. Hamburg. 1839,*

---

This species of *Cyrtanthus* belongs to the same group as the species figured on Plate 25 (*C. sanguineus*). The group is characterised by having a single flower or few flowers in each umbel. Our previous illustrations of *Cyrtanthus* should be compared with the above two and the present plate. *C. helictus*, which is an exceptionally graceful representative of the genus, has not been extensively collected by botanists, and we know of its occurrence in the Somerset East, Graaff Reinet, Fort Beaufort, and Queenstown Divisions only. It should certainly engage the attention of cultivators of South African plants, as it is well worthy of a place in the bulb garden.

Our illustration was made from specimens collected by Dr. E. P. Phillips near Fort Beaufort; these flowered at the Division of Botany in November 1922.

DESCRIPTION:—Bulb 2·7 cm. in diameter, globose, with papery tunics and thick wrinkled roots from the base. *Leaves* contemporary with the flowers, about 3 to each bulb, spirally twisted, 12 cm. long, 4·5 mm. broad, linear, obtuse, narrowed to the base, glabrous. *Peduncle* arising at side of the leaves, 9 cm. long, but sometimes longer, terete, glabrous. *Spathe* valves 2·5 cm.

long, acuminate from an ovate base, membranous. *Flowers* usually solitary. *Pedicel* 1·2 cm. long, terete, glabrous, shorter than the spathe-valves. *Perianth-tube* 3 cm. long, 2 mm. in diameter, and curved at the base, widening to 1·3 cm. in diameter at the throat; lobes 2 cm. long, 9 mm. broad, obovate, obtuse, or the outer segments bluntly apiculate with a pendulous appendage, 5-nerved. *Stamens* in 2 series: the lower with filaments 1·1 cm. long; the upper with filaments 8 mm. long, all filiform; anthers 3·5 mm. long, linear. *Ovary* 7 mm. long, ellipsoid, glabrous; style 5·5 cm. long; lobes 5 mm. long, linear (National Herb. Pretoria 2634).

---

PLATE 99.—Fig. 1, perianth laid open; Fig. 2, perianth lobes; Fig. 3, upper portion of style.

F.P.S.A., 1923.

K. A. Lansdell del

## K. A. LANSDELL DEL

# PLATE 100.

*PROTEA STOKOEI.*

*Cape Province.*

PROTEACEAE. *Tribe* PROTEEAE.

*PROTEA, Linn.; Benth. et Hook. f. Gen. Plant.*

**Protea Stokoei,** *Phillips,* sp. nov. a *P. speciosa,* Linn., aristis calycis subequalibus, et pilis apice bractearum brevioribus differt.

*Rami glabri. Folia* 7-9 cm. longa, 3-4 cm. lata, obovata vel obovato-oblonga, glabra. *Capitulum* sessile, 10-11 cm. longum, 5·5 cm. latum. *Involucri bracteae* 9-10-seriatae; exteriores 1·5-2 cm. longae, ovato-oblongae, apice rotundatae, dense pubescentes, apice barbatae; interiores 9 cm. longae, 2·5 cm. latae, spathulatae, sericeo-pubescentes, infra glabrae, apice barbatae. *Receptaculum* 2 cm. longum, conicum. *Perianthi tubus* 5·5 cm. longus, basi dilatatus; laminae 1·2 cm. longae, villosae; apice triaristatae; aristae laterales 1·8 cm. longae, villosae, media 1·5 cm. longa. *Stamina* 8 mm. longa, linearia, apice glandibus linearibus instructa. *Ovarium* pilis longis vestitum; stylus 6 cm. longus; stigma 6 mm. longum.

This species of *Protea* was collected early in 1921 by Mr. T. P. Stokoe. At the time there was some doubt about its identity, and it was provisionally placed under *P. speciosa*. Recently we received more and better material from the same collector, and have no hesitation in describing it as a species allied to *P. speciosa*. It differs from this species in having shorter tufts of hairs at the apices of the involucral bracts and the awns of the perianth are much longer and subequal. The species belongs to a section of the genus *Speciosae*, which is characterised by having the inner involucral bracts fringed with long hairs or bearded. A comparison should be made with Plates 22, 76 and 84, which illustrate examples of other sections of the genus.

The first specimens collected by Mr. Stokoe came from an isolated krantz on a peak directly opposite Kogelberg on the land side, and subsequently he found specimens also on high peaks facing Kogelberg, but on the seaward side. It probably does not occur lower than an altitude of 3000 ft. The plant is a spreading bush about 6 ft. high (not so compact as *P. speciosa*), and grows with such moisture-loving plants as *Mimetes hottentotica* and *M. splendens*. The young leaves have a fringe of longish white hairs.

DESCRIPTION:—*Branches* glabrous. *Leaves* 7-9 cm. long, 3-4 cm. broad, obovate, obovate-oblong, more rarely elliptic-lanceolate, rounded and slightly emarginate at the apex, slightly narrowed to the base, leathery, with reddish margins, quite glabrous. *Head* sessile, 10-11 cm. long, 5·5 cm. in diameter. *Involucral bracts* 9-10-seriate; the outermost 1·5-2 cm. long, ovate-oblong, rounded at the apex, densely silky pubescent, ciliate with white hairs with a small tuft of brown hairs at the apex; the innermost 9 cm. long, 2·5 cm. broad above, spathulate, silky pubescent, except at the base, with a fringe of dark-brown hairs at the apex about 3 mm. long. *Receptacle* 2 cm. long, conical. *Perianth-sheath* 5·5 cm. long, dilated and 3-keeled below, glabrous; lip 1·2 cm. long, shortly but densely villous, 3-awned; lateral awns 1·8 cm. long, linear, acuminate, shortly but densely villous, tipped with a few brown hairs; median awn 1·5 cm. long, otherwise similar. *Stamens* all fertile; anthers 8 mm. long, linear, with a pink linear apical gland. *Ovary* covered with long, golden-brown hairs; style 6 cm. long, subterete, slightly curved, very sparsely pilose below; stigma 6 mm. long, linear; scarcely bent at junction with style (Type in National Herb. Pretoria, No. 2632).

PLATE 100.—Fig. 1, receptacle; Fig. 2, complete flower; Fig. 3, lamina showing the three awns and stamens; Fig. 4, pistil; Fig. 5, apex of style and stigma.

F.P.S.A., 1923.

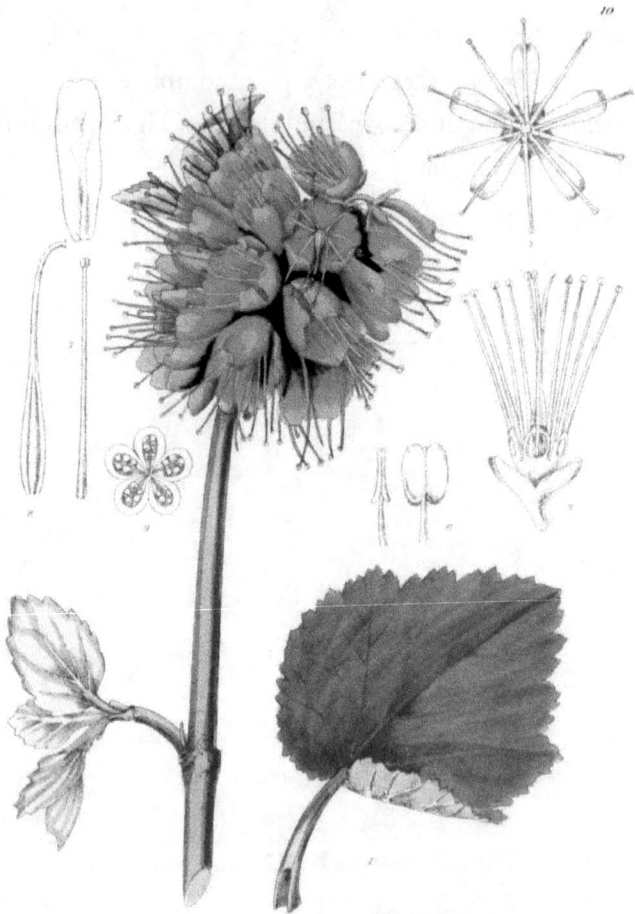

S. GOWER DEL.

# PLATE 101.

*GREYIA* RADLKOFERI
*Transvaal.*

SAPINDACEAE. *Tribe* MELIANTHEAE.

*GREYIA, Hook. et Harv.; Benth. et Hook. f. Gen. Plant.*
**Greyia Radlkoferi**, *Szyszy. Pl. Rehmann.*

An extremely ornamental shrub found in the eastern Transvaal, where it has been recorded from Waterval Onder, 'Thlatikulu and Barberton. The plant does quite well at Pretoria, where specimens have been planted on Meintjes Kop behind the Union Buildings.

The genus *Greyia*, which contains only three known species, was named in honour of Sir George Grey, K.C.B. In South Africa it has a very limited distribution, and is interesting botanically, as there are still some doubts as to its affinities.

In the Transvaal the plant flowers from July to October, the young leaves appearing at the same time as the scarlet flowers. The flowers are proterandrous, *i. e.*, the pollen is shed before the pistil has quite matured, and this makes self-pollination almost impossible.

The Cape species, *Greyia Sutherlandi*, is commonly known as "Baakhout" or "Wild bottlebrush," so that our plant might be appropriately named the "Transvaal Baakhout." The material from which our illustration was made was gathered by Miss S. Gower on Meintjes Kop, Pretoria.

For a roller account of this interesting genus the reader is referred to a paper by Dr. S. Schonland in the *Records of the Albany Museum*, vol. iii. p. 40.

DESCRIPTION:—A shrub 2-5 m. high. *Branches* with light-brown bark, glabrous. *Leaves* at the apex of the branches at the side of the flowers; blade 3·5-12 cm. long, ovate, subacute, cordate at the base, with lobed margins, sparsely pilose above with curled hairs, white-tomentose beneath; petioles 2-10 cm. long, terete, glandular-pilose. *Inflorescence* of many inverted scarlet flowers. *Bracts* 7 mm. long, boat-shaped, glandular-pilose. *Pedicels* 7 mm. long, terete, glandular-pilose. *Calyx-tube* 2 mm. long; lobes 5 mm. long, oblong, shortly apiculate, sparsely glandular-pilose. *Petals* not all equal, 2-2·3 cm. long, almost 1 cm. broad, oblong-obovate, usually rounded at the apex, more rarely emarginate. *Stamens* usually 10, sometimes 8, in two whorls; filaments 2·7 cm. long, terete; anthers 1·5 mm. long, ovate. *Disc* cupular below with 10 or 8 arms from the rim of the cup, each arm has a peltate disc. *Ovary* about 1 cm. long, terete; style 1·8 cm. long, terete; stigma simple. (National Herb. Pretoria, No. 2635.)

---

PLATE 101.—Fig. 1, leaf; 2, flower with petals removed showing disc; 3, ground plan of flower; 4, sepal; 5, petal; 6, anthers front and side view; 7, stamen; 8, pistil; 9, section through the ovary.

F.P.S.A., 1923.

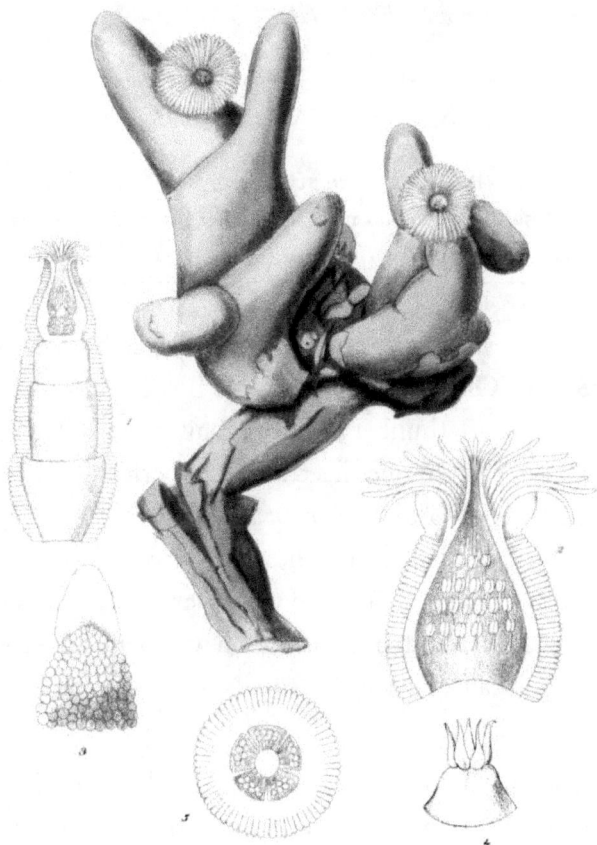

*102*

K A LANSDELL DEL

# PLATE 102.

*MESEMBRYANTHEMUM DIGITATUM.*
*Cape Province.*

FICOIDEAE. TRIBE MESEMBRYEAE.

*MESEMBRYANTHEMUM, Linn.; Benth. et Hook. f. Gen. Plant.*
**Mesembryanthemum digitatum**, *Ait. Hort. Kew. ed.*
*(1789); M. digitiforme, Thunb. in Acad. Leop.-Car. Ephem.*

This curious *Mesembryanthemum* was first collected by Carl Thunberg between the Oliphants River and the Bokkeveld Mountains about 150 years ago. Thunberg described his plant in 1789, and in his herbarium there is one sheet with two perfect growths and two flowers upon it. Marloth (*Flora of South Africa*, Pl. 49) figures a small portion of a plant which, he states, was collected at Van Rhynsdorp by Mr. W. Spilhaus and was as large as a child's head. The specimens from which our illustration was made were collected in the same locality by Mr. E. Rood and sent to the Division of Botany, Pretoria.

The corpuscula, which are very succulent, show an extremely interesting structure when examined in detail. If a longitudinal section is made, a hard green central core is seen, which is the stem; this is surrounded by long, crystalline cells, and the whole covered in by a juicy tissue. As the green tissue is buried in the stem, it is very probable that the crystalline cells referred to act as lenses and concentrate any light which penetrates the outer tissue on to the chlorophyll-bearing cells. The fleshy leaves are almost devoid of chlorophyll.

The flower is borne at the apex of the stem, but this can only be satisfactorily seen in a longitudinal section. The crystalline cells are continued round the base of the calyx.

DESCRIPTION:—Acaulescent plant with woody underground stems and fleshy aerial stems and leaves. *Stems* 2-3 cm. long, 2-2·5 cm. in diameter, very succulent, glabrous. *Leaves* two to each stem, usually one larger than the other, 1·5-2 cm. long, 0·8-1·3 cm. in diameter, terete, blunt, very succulent, glabrous. *Flowers* white, arising from the apex of the stems but appearing on a casual examination to come from the base of one of the leaves, when expanded 1·2-1·5 cm. in diameter. *Petals* in more than one row; the outermost row connate into definite groups, 7 mm. long, less than 0·5 mm. broad, linear, subacute. *Stamens* in four rows; filaments 1 mm. long, filiform; anthers about 1 mm. long, oblong. *Calyx* covered with crystalline cells; lobes almost membranous, 1 cm. long, 3 mm. broad, oblong, or oblong ovate, obtuse. *Ovary* sunk in tissue of stem, 5-celled, with several stalked ovules with axile placentation; upper portion of ovary cone-shaped tipped with five terete, acute styles each 1 mm. long.

PLATE 102.—Fig. 1, longitudinal section of stem showing sheath of crystalline cells and flower embedded at apex; 2, longitudinal section of flower; 3, sepal; 4, top of ovary showing the five stigmas; 5, cross section of ovary.

F.P.S.A., 1923.

# PLATE 103.

*BRACHYCORYTHIS PUBESCENS.*
*Cape Province. Natal. Swaziland. Transvaal.*

ORCHIDACEAE. Tribe OPHRYDEAE.

*BRACHYCORYTHIS, Lindl.; Benth. et Hook. f. Gen. Plant.*
**Brachycorythis pubescens,** *Harv. Thes.*

The genus *Brachycorythis* is represented in Africa by over twenty species, five of which occur in South Africa, and of these three are endemic. The species described here is known from the Cape Province, Natal, Zululand, Swaziland and the northern Transvaal, and extends into tropical Africa. Its occurrence near Pretoria, in a totally different botanical area, is therefore interesting. Harvey first described the plant from specimens found near Durban by Mr. Sanderson, who stated it was plentiful in the neighbourhood.

This attractive little orchid was collected by General the Rt. Hon. J. C. Smuts on the farm Rietvlei No. 221, at Irene, near Pretoria, at an altitude of about 5000 ft. above sea-level. The plant was found in open grassland in deep red loam soil. It has large spreading finger-like tubers and slightly scented flowers.

DESCRIPTION:—A herbaceous plant with long finger-like tubers about 1 cm. thick. *Stem* with inflorescence up to 50 cm. high. *Leaves* erect, crowded 6 cm. long, 3·2 cm. broad at the base of the stem, becoming smaller above, ovate, acuminate, shortly cuspidate, clasping at the base, with the midrib prominent beneath, densely pubescent, with the margins shortly ciliated and

73

somewhat undulate. *Inflorescence* up to 17 cm. long, racemose, many-flowered. *Bracts* similar to the leaves but smaller. *Upper sepal* 5 mm. long, 3 mm. broad, elliptic, rounded above, concave, sparsely pubescent without; lateral sepals 4 mm. long, 2·5 mm. broad, oblong, unequal sided, rounded above, concave, sparsely pubescent without. *Lateral* petals 6 mm. long, 3·5 mm. broad, oblong, rounded above, concave, unequal sided. *Lip* 9 mm. long, 7 mm. broad, obovate, 3-lobed, the middle lobe smaller than the two lateral lobes, narrowed in the middle and then expanded to form a deep pouch. *Anther cells* parallel; pollinia granular, each attached to a separate gland.

---

PLATE 103.—Fig. 1, lower part of plant showing tubers; 2, flower (enlarged); 3, median longitudinal section of flower; 4, sepals; 5, petal; 6, lip; 7, column showing pollinia sacs; 8, pollinium.

F.P.S.A., 1923.

# PLATE 104.

*MACKAYA BELLA.*
*Natal.*

---

ACANTHACEAE. Tribe JUSTICEAE.

*MacKaya, Harv.; Benth. et Hook. f. Gen. Plant.*
**MacKaya bella**, *Harv. Thes.*

---

This plant was discovered in Natal by Mr. J. Sanderson, who sent living specimens to Kew, where it flowered first in May 1869. From the material a figure of the plant was published in the *Botanical Magazine* of the same year. This figure, however, does not accurately represent the plant as it is known in its native habitat and in local cultivation. The flowers are lilac, and not almost white, as indicated in the *Botanical Magazine*. The late Dr. Medley Wood reproduced a pencil drawing of the plant in "Natal Plants" in 1912, and states it "is a handsome shrub, but it is of no economic value; it is found only in the coast and midland districts of Natal, and does not seem to be very common." *MacKaya bella* differs from *Crossandra Greenstockii* (see Plate 77), which also belongs to the *Acanthaceae*, in having almost a regular, not a 1-lipped corolla.

Dr. Harvey, who first described the genus, dedicated it to Dr. J. T. MacKay, keeper of the Dublin University Botanic Garden. Our figure was prepared from plants growing in the "Flanagan Arboretum," Union Buildings, Pretoria.

DESCRIPTION:—A shrub about 1-1·5 m. high. *Branches* pubescent. *Leaves* opposite, petioled; blade 3-6 cm. long, 1·3-3·5 cm. broad, elliptic or elliptic-lanceolate, acuminate, obtuse, usually narrowed at the base, margins lobulate or subentire, with the nerves distinct beneath, glabrous; petioles about 1 cm. long, pubescent. *Flowers* opposite in a terminal lax raceme; the internodes almost 2 cm. long. *Bracts* 4·5 mm. long, subulate; bracteoles 2, at the base of the pedicels. *Pedicel* 5-7 mm. long, pubescent. *Calyx* divided almost to the base; lobes 8 mm. long, acuminate from a base 1 mm. broad, very finely pubescent, and ciliate on the margins. *Corolla-tube* 3·5 cm. long, 2 cm. in diameter at the throat, campanulate above, becoming cylindric below, finely pubescent; lobes 2 cm. long, 1-1·5 cm. broad, ovate, obtuse, very finely pubescent or glabrous. *Fertile stamens* two; filaments fixed to narrow portion of corolla-tube, 1·5 cm. long, terete, with a few scattered short stiff hairs; anthers 7 mm. long, bluntly sagittate at the base, hirsute on the back; sterile stamens represented by filaments only. *Ovary* 3 mm. long, 2-celled, with 2 superposed ovules in each cell, glabrous; style 3·3 cm. long, filiform, with a few scattered hairs at the base; stigma shortly bifid. (National Herb. Pretoria, No. 2638.)

PLATE 104.—Fig. 1, calyx; 2, corolla; 3, anther back view and filament; 4, anther front view; 5, ovary; 6, apex of style showing shortly bifid stigma; 7, longitudinal section of ovary.

F.P.S.A., 1923.

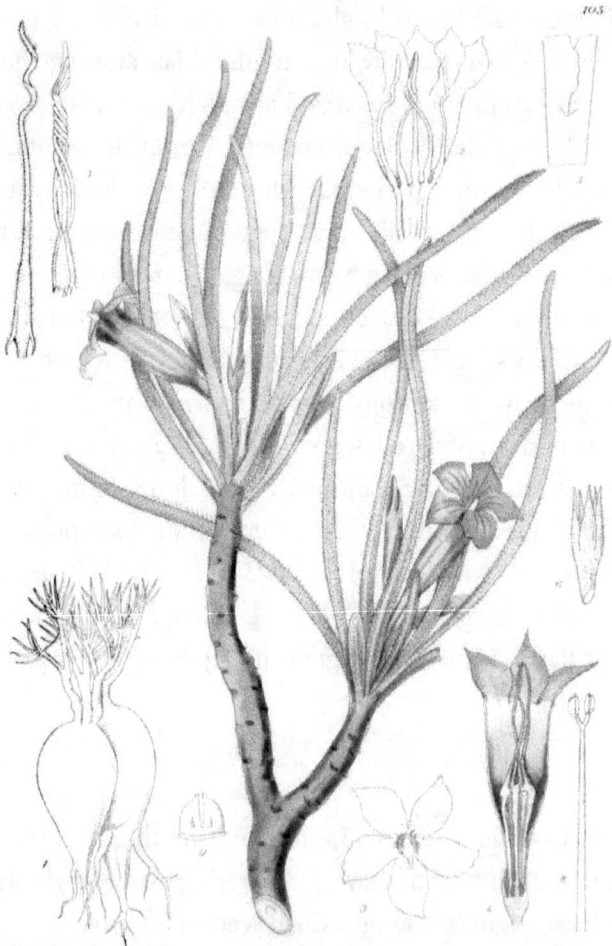

S. GOWER DEL.

# PLATE 105.

*ADENIUM OLEIFOLIUM.*
*Transvaal. Cape Province.*

Apocynaceae. Tribe Echitideae.

*ADENIUM, Roem. et Schult.; Benth. et Hook. f. Gen. Plant.*
**Adenium oleifolium**, *Stapf, var. angustifolium,*
*Phillips var. nov., a typo foliis angustis differt.*

The genus *Adenium* is represented in South Africa by three species found in the Transvaal, Swaziland and the North-Western Cape Province. Species of the genus are also found extending through tropical Africa to Socotra. On Plate 16 we figured *Adenium multiflorum*, from which the present plant differs in having long narrow leaves; both, however, have very large tuberous underground stems from which the branches arise. The peculiar tailed anthers and the scales in the corolla-throat which sometimes form small pouches are characteristic of the genus.

Specimens were submitted to Kew for confirmation of the name, and the Director reports "very probably *A. oleifolium*, Stapf, but leaves are much narrower than in the type," and it was thought advisable to describe this as a narrow-leaved variety.

Our plate was prepared from specimens collected by Dr. W. M. Borcherds at Upington, and forwarded by him to the Division of Botany, Pretoria.

Description:—Plant with large underground tuberous stems from which the branches arise. *Branches* densely pubescent when young, at length becoming glabrous. *Leaves* crowded at the ends of the branches, 6-10 cm. long, 2-4 mm. broad, linear, acute, pubescent. *Flowers* terminal. *Sepals* 6·5 mm. long, ovate, acuminate, acute, densely pilose, united at the base. *Corolla-tube* 3·5 cm. long, cylindric and 3 mm. in diameter in lowest third, campanulate and 1·1 cm. in diameter in uppermost ⅔, pubescent without and within and with pockets in the angles formed by the lobes; lobes 1·3 cm. long, 8-9 mm. broad, broadly-elliptic, acuminate, sub-acute, minutely ciliate. *Filaments* 4 mm. long, thick, terete, densely pilose; anthers 4 mm. long, hairy on the backs, sagittate at the base and produced into a long coiled apical hairy appendage 1 cm. long. *Ovary* 2 mm. long, 2 mm. broad, glabrous, separating into 2 carpels; style 1·6 cm. long, cylindric, glabrous; stigmas 3 mm. long, lanceolate, subacuminate, with a mass of glandular hairs at the back which fix the stigmas to the connective of the anthers. (National Herb. Pretoria, No. 2598.)

---

PLATE 105.—Fig. 1, plant reduced; 2, corolla laid open; 3, corolla from above; 4, pocket in corolla; 5, calyx; 6, stamens; 7, style and stigma; 8, carpels; 9, median longitudinal section of flower.

F.P.S.A., 1923.

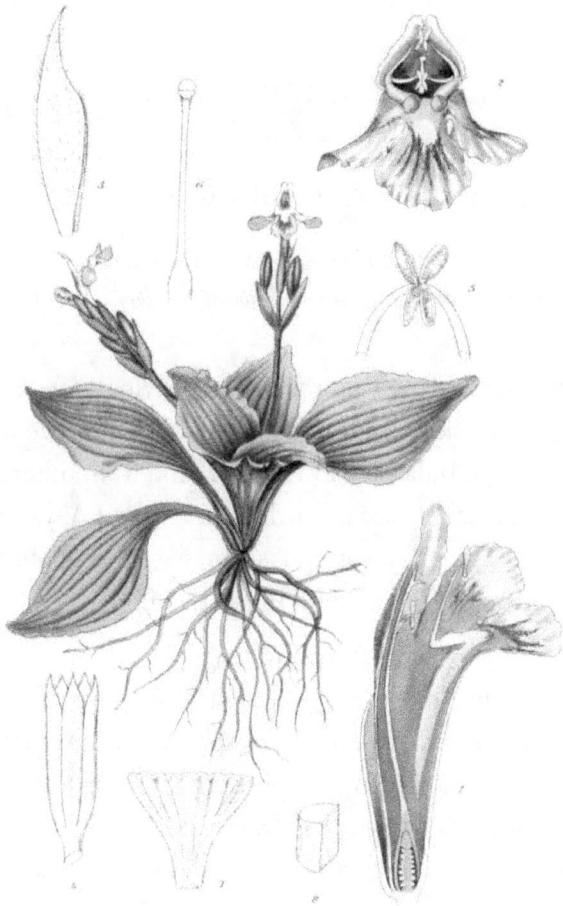

S. GOWER DEL.

# PLATE 106.

*CRATEROSTIGMA PLANTAGINEUM.*
*Transvaal.*

Scrophulariaceae. Tribe Gratioleae.

*CRATEROSTIGMA, Hochst.; Benth. et Hook. f. Gen. Plant.*
**Craterostigma plantagineum**, *Hochst. in Flora, 1841, 669; Fl.*

The *Craterostigma* figured on the accompanying plate is known from various localities in the Transvaal. It is also recorded from the neighbourhood of Bulawayo in Rhodesia and from other parts of tropical Africa reaching as far north as Arabia and Abyssinia. The genus is mainly a tropical one, and is represented by about a dozen species, three of which are found in South Africa.

*C. plantagineum* is a charming little plant which would be well worth cultivation in the greenhouse and should be easily grown. Our plate was prepared from specimens collected by Dr. I. B. Pole Evans, C.M.G., on the portion of the farm Rietfontein 448, near Pretoria, belonging to Mr. J. F. Ludorf. The plants were found growing in great profusion in shallow soil not more than one inch deep on a large quartzite outcrop. They were in flower during November and December.

Description:—An acaulescent plant with a rosette of radical leaves. *Leaves* 6-6·5 cm. long, 3-3·5 cm. broad (the inner smaller), ovate, obtuse, narrowed at the base, with crenulate, ciliated margins and with the nerves depressed above, prominent beneath, glabrous above, pubescent beneath, especially on the veins. *Peduncles* 3 or more to a plant, 3·5-4 cm. long, terete, pubescent, bearing about 8 opposite flowers in a raceme. *Bracts* 1 cm. long, 5 mm. broad, ovate-lanceolate, acute, slightly connate at the base, glabrous except on the keel, ciliate. *Pedicel* 7 mm. long, flat on the upper surface, convex on the lower surface, pubescent, ciliate. *Calyx-tube* 4·5 mm. long, 2·5 mm. in diameter, deeply fluted, pubescent; lobes 1 mm. long, ovate, sub-acute, ciliated. *Corolla* 2-lipped; tube 7 mm. long, tubular; lower lip 9 mm. long, 1 cm. broad, 3-lobed, with the lobes obovate, crenulate; upper lip 7 mm. long, oblong-ovate, bilobed at the apex. *Stamens* of two different kinds; those attached to the lower lip with filaments 7 mm. long, bent at right angles below and then swollen to form two callosities on the lip; those attached to the upper lip 2 mm. long; anther cells diverging, those of each pair of stamens joined. *Ovary* 2 mm. long, 1·25 mm. in diameter, ovoid; style 8 mm. long, terete, gradually widening above, glabrous; stigma bilobed, with the lobes broadly ovate and somewhat membranous. (National Herb. Pretoria, No. 2644.)

---

PLATE 106.—Fig. 1, median longitudinal section of flower; 2, front view of flower enlarged; 3, bract; 4, calyx; 5, stamens; 6, pistil; 7, lower portion of under surface of leaf; 8, section of pedicel snowing convex and flat surfaces.

F.P.S.A., 1923.

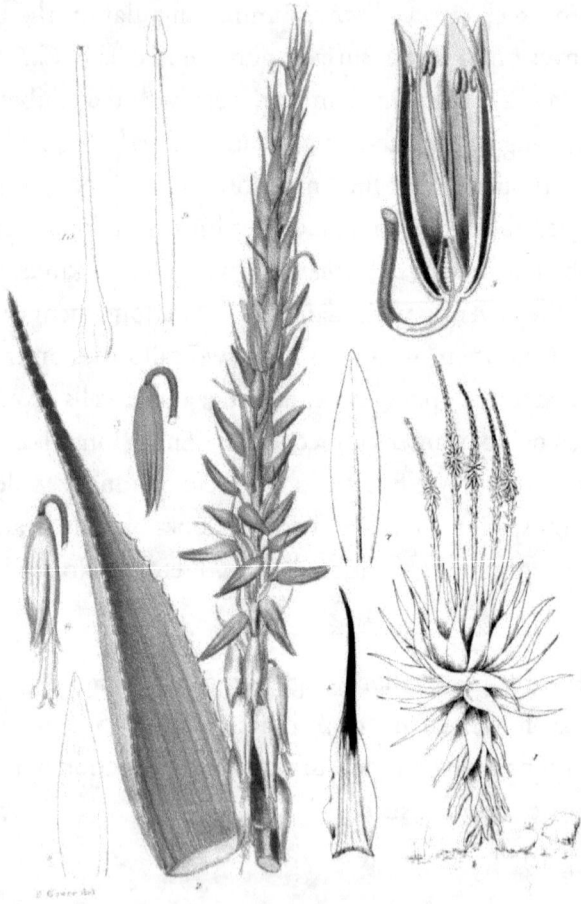

S. GOWER DEL.

# PLATE 107.

*ALOE* COMOSA.
*Cape Province.*

LILIACEAE. *Tribe* ALOINEAE.

*ALOE, Linn.; Benth. et Hook. f. Gen. Plant.*
**Aloe comosa**, *Marloth and A. Berg. in Engl. Bot. Jahrb.*

The Aloe which forms the subject of this plate is, so far as is known, only found on the Bokkeveld beds in the Clanwilliam and Van Rhynsdorp Districts of the Cape Province. Full-grown plants attain a height of 12-15 ft., and when in full bloom, which is usually during December and January, their long massive inflorescences make such a display of colour in the veld that they cannot fail to attract the notice of the traveller. As will be seen from the illustration, the uppermost flowers are hidden by the long bracts, the flowers in the middle portion of the inflorescence are pink and spreading, while those at the base are pendulous and greenish-white. The stamens are only exserted from the pendulous flowers, and after pollination the filaments contract and are withdrawn into the perianth, which closes round them, leaving the style exserted. This phenomenon is also found in *Aloe saponaria* figured on Plate 96, and is probably fairly general in the genus *Aloe*.

The material from which our plate was made was collected by Dr. I. B. Pole Evans, C.M.G., on the Doorn River near Van Rhynsdorp, and brought to Pretoria, where the plants flower regularly every year during December and January. *Aloe comosa* was first collected and described by Dr. R. Marloth, who found it between Clanwilliam and Van Rhynsdorp in 1904.

DESCRIPTION:—Plant with a short stout stem or sometimes up to 12 ft. bearing a rosette of fleshy leaves at the apex, *Leaves* up to 52 cm. long, 10 cm. broad in the widest part, ovate-lanceolate, acuminate, acute, flat above, slightly convex beneath, deeply channelled on the upper surface above, with the veins somewhat distinct on the upper surface and with the margins covered with sharp teeth; teeth 5-7 mm. apart, 2 mm. long, ovate. *Inflorescence* lateral about 1·3 m. long, racemose, narrowly cylindric, with the lowermost flowers pendulous, the upper flowers erect and adpressed and the median flowers spreading. *Peduncle* about 60 cm. long, 1·5 cm. in diameter, terete, covered with long membranous ovate-acuminate bracts 5 cm. long, 1 cm. broad. *Floral-bracts* 6 cm. long, lanceolate, long acuminate, acute, with membranous margins, encircling the pedicel. *Pedicel* 1·8-2 cm. long, at first erect, at length becoming curved, terete. *Perianth-tube* 1·2 cm. long, campanulate; outer lobes grenadine-pink, 2 cm. long, 5 mm. broad, lanceolate, hooded at the apex, 3-nerved; inner lobes whitish, 2 cm. long, obtuse and hooded at the apex, 1-nerved. *Filaments* 1·8 cm. long, lengthening to 4 cm. long in old flowers; anthers 3 mm. long, oblong. *Ovary* ellipsoid; style 2 cm. long, lengthening to 4 cm. in old flowers; stigma simple with a ring of papillose hairs. (National Herb. Pretoria, No. 2643.)

---

PLATE 107.—Fig. 1, entire plant much reduced; 2, inflorescence × ⅔; 3, leaf × ⅔; 4, median longitudinal section of flower; 5, bract; 6, young flower; 7, mature flower with stamens exserted; 8, inner perianth segment; 9, outer perianth segment.

F.P.S.A., 1923.

S. GOWER DEL.

# PLATE 108.

*PROTEA PITYPHYLLA VAR. LATIFOLIA.*
*Cape Province.*

PROTEACEAE. Tribe PROTEAE.

*PROTEA, Linn.; Benth. et Hook. f. Gen. Plant.*
**Protea pityphylla**, *Phill. var. latifolia,*
*Phillips var. nov., a typo foliis latis differt.*

The *Protea* figured on the accompanying plate is readily distinguished from the species by its flat, linear leaves, and on this character alone has been described as a variety of *P. pityphylla*, Phill. We are indebted to Miss L. Guthrie of the Bolus Herbarium for the specimens, which she received from Mr. de Wet of Ceres. The plant is stated to grow in the same habitat and to be found associated with *P. pityphylla* and *P. Marlothii*. It has the characteristic involucre of the former species, namely, the long leaf-like appendages from the apices of the lowermost bracts and also the same pendulous heads. The section of the genus (§ *Pinifoliæ*), comprising species with narrowly linear, filiform or needle-shaped leaves, to which this plant belongs is illustrated here for the first time.

DESCRIPTION:—*Branches* glabrous. *Leaves* 5·5-6·5 cm. long, 3 mm. broad, linear, bluntly apiculate, slightly narrowed to the base, glabrous. *Head* sessile, 4·5 cm. long, about 6·5 cm. in diameter, cernuous. *Involucral-bracts* 7-8-seriate, glabrous; the outer ovate, obtuse, sometimes subacuminate, minutely ciliate, the lowermost produced into long foliaceous appendages resembling the leaves; inner 3·5 cm. long, 1·3 cm. broad, concave, arching over and exceeding the flowers. *Perianth-sheath* 2 cm. long, dilated and 3-keeled below, setulose on the uppermost portion, otherwise glabrous; lip 5·5 mm. long, 3-toothed, 3-keeled, setulose below; teeth subequal, ·5 mm. long, the middle tooth smaller than the two lateral. *Filaments* ·5 mm. long; anthers 3·5 mm. long, linear, with an ovate fleshy apical gland less than ·5 mm. long. *Ovary* covered with long golden hairs; style over 2·5 cm. long, widened and much compressed at the base, sickle-shaped, glabrous; stigma 4 mm. long, scarcely swollen at the junction with the style, obtuse. (National Herb. Pretoria, No. 2586.)

---

PLATE 108.—Fig. 1, receptacle; 2, unopened flower; 3, flower with perianth segments separated; 4, base of style showing the flattened portion.

F.P.S.A., 1923.

*109.*

S. GOWER DEL.

# PLATE 109.

*TRIASPIS NELSONI.*
*Transvaal.*

MALPIGHIACEAE. *Tribe* HIRRAE.

TRIASPIS, *Burch.; Benth. et Hook. f. Gen. Plant.*
**Triaspis Nelsoni**, *Oliv. in Hook. Ic. Pl. t. 1418.*

*Triaspis Nelsoni* was first described and figured in 1883 from material collected by Mr. W. Nelson at Pretoria. The figure given by Hooker is incorrect in a few small details. The pedicels, for instance, are articulated and bear 2 small bracteoles; the three styles are not equal, but one is longer than the other two and is deflexed at an angle of about 45°; the anterior petal is exterior in the bud and larger than the other petals.

The genus Triaspis is found in Madagascar, tropical and southern Africa, and was first recorded by the famous traveller Burchell, who collected specimens of a plant he described as *T. hypericoides* at Kosi Fountain in Bechuanaland in 1812. Since then several species have been recorded from the Transvaal.

The species figured on the accompanying plate is of frequent occurrence on the soils overlying the dolomite outcrops south of Pretoria at an elevation of 4000-5000 ft. above sea-level. It forms a subherbaceous bush not more than two feet high, and the main branches always tend to droop. When in flower it is a most attractive and beautiful object in the veld, and is well worth cultivation in our gardens. In addition to the beauty of its flowers, its large copper-coloured orbicular winged fruits add considerably to its charm and gracefulness. The material from which our plate was prepared was collected by Dr. I. B. Pole Evans, C.M.G., on the farm Doornkloof, Irene, near Pretoria, belonging to General the Rt. Hon. J. C. Smuts.

DESCRIPTION:—A subherbaceous plant with long slender and graceful branches from an underground rootstock. *Branches* terete, pubescent. *Leaves* opposite, decussate, 2-3 cm. long, 1-2·2 cm. broad, the upper leaves smaller than the lower, ovate, sub-apiculate, cordate at the base, with distinct reticulate veining and with the midrib prominent beneath, sparsely pubescent, with ciliated margins. *Inflorescence* a 5-6-flowered axillary raceme, arranged in the axils of the upper leaves. *Peduncle* 1·3 cm. long, terete, pubescent. *Pedicels* 1·5 cm. long, articulated in the lowermost ⅓, pubescent, bearing 2 small bracts. *Sepals* 3·5 mm. long, 1·5 mm. broad, oblong, rounded above, sparsely pubescent. *Petals* 1 cm. long, 6 mm. broad, concave, oblong, rounded above, produced into a claw at the base, with fimbriated margins; the lowermost petal overlapping the others in bud and larger than the rest. *Stamens* 10; filaments 5 mm. long, glabrous; stamens 2 mm. long, linear-oblong. *Ovary* 2 mm. long, globose, villous; styles 3, two stand erect; the posterior style reflexed and smaller than the other two. *Fruit* 3-winged with the wings deeply saucer-shaped. (National Herb. Pretoria, No. 2642.)

---

PLATE 109.—Fig. 1, bud; 2, median longitudinal section of flower; 3, pistil; 4, fruit..

F.P.S.A., 1923.

S. GOWER DEL.

# PLATE 110.

*MESEMBRYANTHEMUM PILLANSII.*
*Cape Province.*

FICOIDEAE. *Tribe* MESEMBRYEAE.

*Mesembryanthemum, Linn.; Benth. et Hook. f. Gen. Plant.*
**Mesembryanthemum Pillansii**, *Kensit in Plant. Nov.*
*Hort. Then. II. tab. 57 (1908); Botanical Mag. t. 8703.*

Dr. R. Marloth supplies the following interesting note on this plant. "Originally found by Mr. Eustace Pillans (not Mr. N. Pillans, as stated in the *Botanical Magazine*) on the farm Mouton Valley on the Piquetberg mountains to the north-west of Piquetberg.

The present plants were gathered by me at the same locality in October 1922 on sandstone hills among *Protea* trees (waabom, *P. grandiflora*), forming shrublets 1½ to 2 ft. high with erect virgate branches.

The description in the *Botanical Magazine* is fairly correct, but the coloured petals are all radiating on the wild plants (not some erect and conniving, as stated in the *Botanical Magazine* for the cultivated plants). They are arranged in 5 groups in front of the sepals. The stigmata are distinct and papillate in the later stages of the flower.

The plant is easily cultivated at Cape Town, and I have had it in flower for several years from September to December.

The flowers are of special biological interest. The stamens do not stand erect as in most other species, but are incurved towards the centre to such an extent that the filaments from opposite stamens meet and the anthers are consequently enclosed in the lentil-shaped cavity thus formed above the concave apex of the ovary. The roof of this cavity is further strengthened by the filiform white inner petals which possess a rough surface and are also tightly incurved inwards, meeting at the centre.

The pollen is produced in profusion, and a mass of white powder is found in every flower when slit open at this stage. In all the flowers examined by me I found a number of small black beetles not more than 2 mm. long and a few specimens of haplothrips, all thoroughly covered with pollen. These insects are able to force their way in between the filaments and inner petals, but cannot escape until the stamens wither. Up to that time no stigmatic surfaces are visible in the centre of the flower, but within a few days, when the flower is about a week old and when the pollen at first accumulated in the concave apex of the ovary has been blown away by the wind, the stigmas develop to a length of 2-3 mm., showing a papillate surface, and are then in a condition to be cross-pollinated by the insects released from flowers in the first stage."

DESCRIPTION:—A succulent plant. *Branches* glabrous, angled and somewhat winged. *Leaves* connate 2·8-4 cm. long, ovate, acute, flat above, acutely keeled beneath, with the margins somewhat scarious. *Flowers* terminal, about 4 cm. in diameter when expanded. *Sepals* unequal, ovate, acuminate, acute, two of the sepals have membranous appendages on the inner face. *Petals* 1·7 cm. long, obovate, produced into a long claw. *Stamens* bending over into cavity of receptacle; filaments linear. *Stigmas* sessile on floor of receptacle. (National Herb. Pretoria, No. 2646.)

PLATE 110.—Fig. 1, median longitudinal section of flower with sepals and petals removed; 2, sepals; 3, petal enlarged; 4, stamen; 5, cross section of ovary; 6, fruit; 7, section of leaf.

F.P.S.A., 1923.

S. GOWER DEL.

# PLATE 111.

*ALOE* MICROCANTHA.

*Cape Province, Swaziland, Transvaal.*

LILIACEAE. *Tribe* ALOINEAE.

*ALOE, Linn.; Benth. et Hook. f. Gen. Plant.*
**Aloe microcantha**, *Haw. Suppl. 105; Fl. Sims in Bot. Mag. t. 2272.*

*Aloe microcantha*, which forms the subject of the accompanying plate, occurs frequently in the open grass veld along the eastern mountain range from Grahamstown northwards as far as the valley of the Limpopo. In Swaziland and the eastern Transvaal it is usually found along the edges of streams and in marshy places. In localities of high rainfall, such as Haenertsberg on the Drakensbergen in the Transvaal, this plant is often a conspicuous and beautiful object on the grassy slopes facing east. It flowers during January and February. As soon as the seed has set, a few months later, the leaves wither almost completely to their bases, leaving a short stem surrounded by a few dried leaves to weather the winter drought.

We are indebted to Mr. Chas. Maggs of Pretoria for the specimen figured in our illustration. It was collected by Mr. Maggs on his Waterval Estate, near Sabie, on the Drakensberg, in January 1921, and forwarded to the Division of Botany, where it flowered in January the following year.

*Aloe microcantha* was first collected by Bowie and introduced into cultivation in 1819. It was figured in Curtis' *Botanical*

*Magazine* in 1821 as a plant of great rarity from the Cape of Good Hope.

DESCRIPTION:—An acaulescent plant. *Leaves* up to 33 cm. long, 4·5 cm. broad at the base, lanceolate, acuminate, acute, concave, sparsely covered with greenish-white spots near the base and with rigidly ciliated margins. *Inflorescence* about 50 cm. long, terete, glabrous, bearing a few distant membranous ovate acuminate acute bracts. *Inflorescence* congested, corymbose. *Bracts* 1·5 cm. long, ovate, acuminate, acute. *Pedicels* 3 cm. long, terete, glabrous. *Perianth* 2·8 to 3·2 cm. long; lobes 2·7 cm. long, 6 mm. broad, linear, obtuse. *Filaments* 2 cm. long, filiform; anthers linear. *Ovary* 1 cm. long, cylindric; style 2·7 cm. long, filiform; stigma simple. (National Herb. Pretoria, No. 2645.)

---

PLATE 111.—Fig. 1, plant much reduced; 2, median longitudinal section of flower; 3, perianth segments; 4, anther; 5, style; 6, cross-section of leaf about the middle.

F.P.S.A., 1923.

K. A. LANSDELL DEL.

# PLATE 112.

*ERYTHRINA HUMEANA.*
*Cape Province, Natal.*

---

LEGUMINOSAE. *Tribe* PHASEOLEAE.

*ERYTHRINA, Linn.; Benth. et Hook. f. Gen. Plant.*
**Erythrina Humeana**, *Spreng. Syst. iii. 243; E.*
*Humei, E. Mey. Comm. Pl. Afr. Austr. 150; Fl.*

---

In a previous issue, on Plate 59, we figured the Kaffir Boom (*Erythrina caffra*), from which the present species differs in being of a dwarf habit and having the nerves of the leaves and petioles covered with prickles. It is a common plant on the slopes of the Drakensberg in Natal, extending southward to Grahamstown, and during the summer months the bright red flowers are very conspicuous in the veld. The leaves of this species, as well as those of *E. caffra*, are attacked by a gall-producing insect, and the seeds are attacked by insects to such an extent that it is difficult to find ripe seed.

The species has been known to cultivators in Europe for over 100 years, and was figured in the *Botanical Magazine* as early as 1823. It is a very handsome shrub which stands from 4 to 8 ft. high, and is well worth cultivation.

DESCRIPTION:—An erect shrub ·9 to 3 m. high. *Stem* and branches terete, ashen-grey, prickly. *Leaves* pinnately trifoliate, 5 to 7·5 cm. long and wide, broadly ovate, gradually narrowing to an acute apex, occasionally very much attenuated and 3-veined at the base; the terminal leaflet similar but smaller and broader in proportion to its length; the midribs of all usually bearing prickles; stipule 6 mm. long, oblong, acute; stipellae glandular. *Petiole* 5 to 7·5 cm. long, with scattered broad-based prickles along its whole length. *Peduncle* 30 to 40 cm. long, terete, bearing flowers in the upper half. *Flowers* crowded. *Calyx* 5-toothed, 1 cm. long, pubescent; tube subcylindric; teeth acute. *Vexillum* 3·7 cm. long, oblong; alae 1 cm. long, oblong; carina 1·1 cm. long, ovate. *Ovary* many-ovuled, tipped with the persistent style. *Legume* 7·5 to 12·5 cm. long, 2-to 5-seeded, torulose with wide spaces between the seeds.

PLATE 112.—Fig. 1, leaf and raceme, natural size; 2, calyx, twice natural size; 3, vexillum; 4, wing; 5, keel; 6, stamens; 7, pistil; 8, pod; 9, portion of branch, much reduced.

F.P.S.A., 1923.

S. GOWER DEL.

# PLATE 113.

*ADENIA DIGITATA.*
*Transvaal.*

PASSIFLORACEAE. *Tribe* MODECCEAE.

*ADENIA, Forsk. Fl. Aegypt. Arab. 77 (1775).*
**Adenia digitata**, *Engl. Bot. Jahrb. Modecca digitata, Harv. Thes.*

The species of *Adenia* described below and figured on the accompanying Plate is of special interest, inasmuch as the large tuberous roots have proved to be extremely poisonous. In October 1922 the plant was brought to the notice of the Division of Botany by Dr. H. Osborne of Pretoria, who reported that two white labourers were admitted to the Pretoria Hospital suspected of having been poisoned by eating a portion of the root, and that one of them died shortly after admission to the Hospital. A sample of the root sent in by Dr. Osborne was submitted to Drs. H. H. Green and W. H. Andrews of the Division of Veterinary Research, and as a result of their investigations two types of poison were discovered. One of these acts very rapidly, and with symptoms which can be attributed to the small amount of a cyanogetic glucoside; the other acts more slowly, but its chemical nature is as yet unknown. A full account of these investigations will be published in the *Report of the Director of Veterinary Research*.

The fruits of *Adenia digitata* are berries of a very attractive nature, and also appear to be poisonous, for some years ago in the Pretoria District two native children died after eating them.

The plant is quite common in the Pretoria District, and also occurs in the Barberton District. It has long, graceful branches provided with tendrils, by means of which it climbs up neighbouring bushes and shrubs.

DESCRIPTION:—*Roots* tuberous, sometimes up to 50 cm. in diameter. *Stems* striate. *Leaves* 8 to 14 cm. long, digitately 3-to 5-lobed; the middle lobe pinnatisect; the side lobes again lobed on one side only or pinnatilobed, more rarely almost entire; the mid-rib prominent above and beneath, and with two prominent glands on the upper side at base of the lamina, and with glands beneath at the base of each leaf-segment, glabrous; petiole 1·3 to 1·7 cm. long, 6 to 7 mm. broad, flat above, convex beneath, glabrous. *Calyx-tube* 1·5 cm. long, campanulate, 1 cm. in diameter above, narrowing to 1·5 mm. in diameter at the base, glabrous; lobes 7 cm. long, 5·5 mm. broad, ovate, obtuse, glabrous; two lobes with entire, the other three with lacerated margins. *Petals* 9 mm. long, 2·5 mm. broad at the widest part, obovate, acuminate, obtuse, narrowed at the base, with shortly ciliated margins, 3-nerved. *Filaments* united at the base, 4 mm. long, linear, broadening at the base; anthers 6·5 mm. long, 1·5 mm. broad, linear, falcate when seen in side view. *Glands* at base of filaments ·5 mm. long, more or less quadrate. *Style* 1 mm. long, bilobed at the apex. *Corona* represented by a fimbriated rim. *Fruit* fleshy, 3·5 cm. long, 2·5 cm. in diameter. *Female flower* not seen. (National Herb. Pretoria, No. 2639.)

---

PLATE 113.—Fig. 1, tuberous root × ½; 2, portion of petiole and bases of leaf-lobes showing glands; 3, flower laid open showing entire and fimbriated sepals; 4, petal; 5, stamens side view; 6, stamen front view; 7, fruit; 8, longitudinal section of fruit showing seeds.

F.P.S.A., 1923.

S. GOWER DEL.

# PLATE 114.

---

HAEMODORACEAE. *Tribe* EUHAEMODOREAE.

WACHENDORFIA, *Linn.; Benth. et Hook. f. Gen. Plant.*
**Wachendorfia paniculata**, *Linn. Sp. Plant. 59; Fl.*

---

This plant is popularly known as "rooi knol," because of the deep red colour of the tubers when cut, and it is also known as "Spinnekop blom," as the colour and marking of the perianth resemble that of some spiders. The latter name is also applied to *Ferraria undulata* (see Plate 66 for an illustration of a species of the genus).

The species was known in England at least as early as 1767, as there is a record of its introduction into Kew Gardens in that year. The dull brown colour of the flowers, which is rare among South African plants, does not make the plant a very ornamental object in gardens, but as the plant is interesting botanically it should have a place in any collection of the native flora.

The family *Haemodoraceae* contains about 120 species, found principally in Australia, but species are also known in North and South America and in Asia. In South Africa the family is represented by less than 50 species, the largest genus being *Sansevieria*. The genus *Wachendorfia* is known by only two species.

Our plate was prepared from plants sent by Mrs. E. Rood, Van Rhynsdorp; they flowered at the Division of Botany in 1922.

DESCRIPTION:—*Rhizomes* a deep red colour when freshly cut.

*Leaves* 5 to 6 to a plant, 16 to 23 cm. long, 1·2 to 1·8 cm. broad, long-lanceolate, acuminate, acute, narrowed below, sheathing at the base with 3 main nerves, glabrous and with ciliated margins. *Peduncle*, including the inflorescence, up to 60 cm. long, glandular-pubescent, with about 3 reduced leaves 5 cm. long, and long-acuminate from a broad base. *Inflorescence* a lax panicle. *Bracts* 1 to 3 cm. long, long acuminate, membranous, distinctly veined, pilose. *Pedicels* ·6 to 1 cm. long, pilose with glandular hairs. *Outer perianth-lobes* 1·7 cm. long, 4·5 mm. broad, oblanceolate, obtuse, many-nerved, pilose outside with glandular hairs; inner lobes 1·7 cm. long, 3·5 mm. broad, oblanceolate, obtuse, membranous, nerved, glabrous. *Filaments* 1·2 cm. long, linear, narrowing above, membranous, with a single vein, glabrous; anthers 2·5 mm. long, oblong. *Ovary* 2 mm. in diameter, bluntly 3-angled, very densely pilose with glandular hairs; style 1·95 cm. long, linear, glabrous; stigma simple. (National Herb. Pretoria, No. 2605.)

---

PLATE 114.—Fig. 1, perianth segment; 2, stamen and single anther; 3, pistil showing side and top view of ovary.

F.P.S.A., 1923.

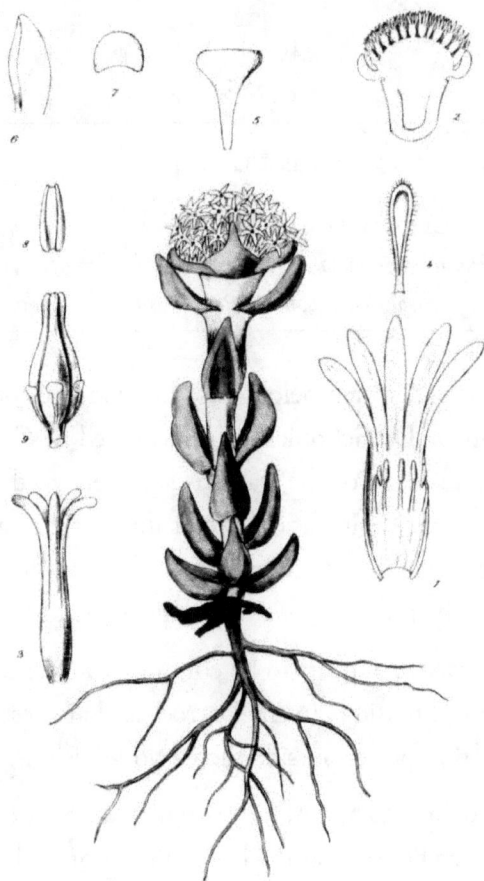

S. GOWER DEL.

# PLATE 115.

*CRASSULA CONGESTA.*
Cape Province.

CRASSULACEAE.

*CRASSULA,* Linn.; Benth. et Hook. f. Gen. Plant.
**Crassula congesta**, N. E. Br. in Gard. Chron. 11 (1902),
C. pachyphylla, Schonl. in Record. Albany Museum

This little *Crassula*, which belongs to the section *Pryamidella*, is, as pointed out by Dr. Schonland, closely allied to *C. columnaris*, Thunb., but the shape of the leaves is sufficient to distinguish it from the latter species. It was described almost simultaneously by Mr. N. E. Brown and Dr. Schonland, but as Brown's description was the first to be published we retain his name for the species.

*Crassula congesta* appears to be confined to the Matjesfontein and Laingsburg Divisions in the Karroo, and at present we have no records of the species outside these two Divisions.

We are indebted to Mr. A. J. Austin of Matjesfontein for living specimens which flowered at the Division of Botany in July 1922.

DESCRIPTION:—Plant succulent, about 9 cm. high. *Stem* glabrous. *Leaves* 1·7 cm. long, up to 2·7 cm. broad, decussate, connate, transversely oblong, convex without, concave within, glabrous. *Heads* many flowered, 2·5 cm. in diameter. *Receptacle* convex. *Floral-bracts* ·5 mm. long, ·75 mm. broad, linear, obtuse; ciliated, membranous. *Calyx-tube* 1 mm. long, glabrous, membranous; lobes 2·5 mm. long, ·5 mm. broad, linear, obtuse, ciliate. *Corolla-tube* 3·5 mm. long, membranous; lobes 5 mm. long, ·75 mm. broad, linear, obtuse. *Filaments* 2 mm. long, filiform; anthers 1·25 mm. long, oblong. *Squamae* 1 mm. long, spatulate and produced into a long claw. *Carpels* 2·5 mm. long, tapering from the base upwards; stigma simple. (National Herb. Pretoria, No. 2602.)

PLATE 115.—Figs. 1, 2, leaf and section of leaf; 3, single flower; 4, corolla opened; 5, sepal; 6, bract; 7, scale; 8, carpels showing scales.

F.P.S.A., 1923.

S. GOWER DEL.

# PLATE 116.

*GLADIOLUS PSITTACINUS.*

*Cape Province, Orange Free State, Transvaal, Natal, Portuguese East Africa.*

IRIDACEAE. Tribe IXIEAE.

*GLADIOLUS, Linn.; Benth. et Hook. f. Gen. Plant.*
**Gladiolus psittacinus**, *Hook. in Bot. Mag. 3032; Fl.*

On Plate 6 we figured a variety of this magnificent species of *Gladiolus*, which differs from our present plant not only in the colouring of the flower, but also in the size of the perianth-segments.

It was figured in the *Botanical Magazine* (t. 3032) from specimens which flowered at Kew, and was known in cultivation in England at least as early as 1830, and in Holland before that date.

A bed of plants growing at the Division of Botany, Pretoria, made an exceptionally fine display this season (1923), and there can be little doubt that it is the finest native *Gladiolus* to be found in South Africa.

The plant is quite easily propagated, and forms new corms very readily. It is commonly known as the "Natal Lily." Our plate was prepared from specimens forwarded by Mr. H. E. Forsyth, the Curator, Municipal Park, Benoni, and were stated to have been collected in Portuguese East Africa.

DESCRIPTION:—*Corm* 3 cm. in diameter, globose, covered with fibrous tunics. *Plant* 1 to 1·5 m. high. *Leaves* 10 to 12 to a plant, equitant, up to 70 cm. long, 2·5 to 3 cm. broad, ensiform, acuminate, acute, with a prominent midrib above and beneath, and with the lateral veins distinct, with a cartilaginous margin which is sometimes very minutely denticulate, glabrous. *Spike* ·3 to almost 1 m. long, up to 15-flowered. *Outer spathe* 8 cm. long, 2·1 cm. broad, ovate, acuminate, acute, closely nerved, glabrous; inner spathe 6 cm. long, 1·8 cm. broad, ovate, acute, 2-keeled, glabrous (in the flowering stage spathes are smaller). *Perianth-tube* 4 cm. long, 1 cm. in diameter above, yellow on the posterior side, red on anterior side. *Upper lobe* 5·5 cm. long, 3·2 cm. broad, obovate, narrowed to the base, shortly cuspidate; side lobes 4·5 cm. long, 3·5 cm. broad, ovate, obtuse; lower lateral lobes 3 cm. long, 1·5 cm. broad, elliptic, narrowed to the base, acuminate, acute; lowest petal 3·5 cm. long, 1·8 cm. broad, elliptic narrowed to the base, cuspidate at the apex. *Anthers* 1·6 cm. long, linear, sagittate at the base. *Style* 7 cm. long, terete, glabrous; lobes 6 cm. long, spatulate, papillose on the margins. *Young fruit* 4·5 cm. long, 3-angled. *Seeds* winged. (National Herb. Pretoria, No. 2711.)

PLATE 116.—Fig. 1, plant much reduced; 2, longitudinal section of flower; 3, outer bract; 4, inner bract; 5, anther with part of filament; 6, stigmas with part of style; 7, young fruit; 8, seed.

F.P.S.A., 1923.

S. GOWER DEL.

# PLATE 117.

*VENIDIUM* MACROCEPHALUM.

*S. W. Africa.*

## COMPOSITAE. Tribe ARCTOTIDEAE.

*VENIDIUM, Less.; Benth. et Hook. f. Gen. Plant.*
**Venidium macrocephalum**, *DC. Prodr. Fl. Bot. Mag.* t. 8845.

Our illustration was made from plants raised at the Division of Botany, Pretoria, from seed collected by Dr. J. M. Troup at Aus in South-west Africa. The plant flowers freely and makes a splendid display, and as a garden plant for supplying cut flowers it is well worth cultivation.

Seed was sent by the Chief of the Division of Botany to Kew in 1918, and the plants raised were figured in the *Botanical Magazine* (t. 8845). Mr. J. Hutchinson, who drew up the description for the *Botanical Magazine*, gives as his reason for retaining this genus separate from *Arctotis* (see Plate 3) that the latter has a well-developed double pappus, whereas in *Venidium* the pappus is either absent or very rudimentary.

The species of *Venidium*, in common with many species of *Gazania, Arctotis* and *Dimorphotheca*, are collectively known as "Gous Bloom."

DESCRIPTION:—A herbaceous sticky plant with radicle leaves. *Leaves* 16 to 19 cm. long lyrate; the uppermost lobe 7 to 8 cm. long, 2·5 to 5 cm. broad, the margins lobed with broad oblong lobes, with three main veins, distinct above and prominent beneath, cobwebby on both surfaces; lower lobes 1 to 2·5 cm. long; ·7 to 1·3 broad, oblong, obtuse, cobwebby above and beneath; petiole flat above, convex beneath, with three distinct keels, scantily cobwebby; cauline leaves 2 to 9 cm. long, pinnatilobed, eared and somewhat clasping at the base. *Stems* up to 33 cm. long, terete, ribbed, covered with long glandular hairs. *Heads* solitary at ends of stems, 8 to 9 cm. in diameter when fully expanded. *Involucral bracts* in 4 rows; outermost 8 mm. long, acuminate from a broad base, green, covered with long glandular hairs; innermost 1·2 cm. long, glabrous, membranous. *Receptacle* 1·5 cm. in diameter, honeycombed, the margins of the cells membranous and produced into long awns. *Ray-floret* female, lemon-chrome, orange at base. *Tube* 3 mm. long, cylindric; lobe 3·5 cm. long, 7 mm. broad, lanceolate, minutely 3-toothed at the apex, 2-keeled beneath; at throat of tube are four minute black structures representing reduced corolla lobes. *Pappus* less than ·5 mm. membranous. *Ovary* 1 mm. long; style 4 mm. long, terete, thickened below the lobes; lobes 1 mm. long, oblong, obtuse. *Disc-florets* hermaphrodite. *Corolla-tube* 3 mm. long, 1·25 mm. in diameter above, slightly narrower at the base, sparsely glandular; lobes 1·5 mm. long, linear, obtuse. *Anthers* black, 2·25 mm. long, blunt at base. *Ovary* and pappus similar to those of ray-florets; style thin for the first 3 mm., then suddenly much thickened in the upper 2 mm. of its length; lobes ·5 mm. long, oblong, obtuse. (National Herb. Pretoria, No. 2599.)

PLATE 117.—Fig. 1, basal leaf reduced; 2, outer involucral bract; 3, inner involucral bract; 4, longitudinal section through receptacle; 5, surface view of part of receptacle; 6, ray-floret; 7, stigmas and portion of style of ray-floret; 8, disc-floret; 9, stigmas and portion of style of disc-floret; 10, fruit.

F.P.S.A., 1923.

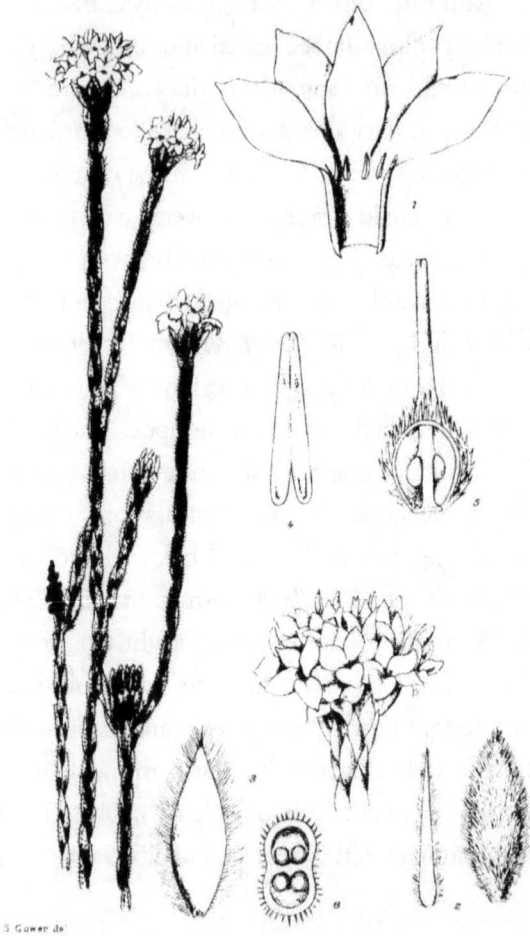

S. GOWER DEL

# PLATE 118.

*LONCHOSTOMA MONOSTYLIS.*
*Cape Province.*

---

BRUNIACEAE.

*LONCHOSTOMA, Wickstr.; Benth. et Hook. f. Gen. Plant.*
**Lonchostoma monostylis**, *Sond. in Harv. et Sond. Fl.*

---

This member of the family *Bruniaceae* differs from that previously figured (*Brunia Stokoei*, Plate 92) in having a tubular corolla. In this respect it is also unique in the family. The genus is a small one, comprising only four known species.

Ecklon and Zeyher collected this plant in the Palmiet River Valley, and since then it has not been recorded until recently, when Mr. T. P. Stokoe gathered it in the same locality. He sent fresh specimens to the Division of Botany, and from these the plate was made.

*Lonchostoma monostylis* is a graceful plant with long, thin, erect stems, at the apex of which the flowers are borne.

DESCRIPTION:—*Stems* simple or sometimes branched above, 40 to 50 cm. long, almost woolly, at length becoming glabrous. *Leaves* erect, adpressed to the branches and almost hiding them, 5 to 6 mm. long, 1·5 to 2 mm. broad, elliptic, obtuse, with a small black mucro, concave, pubescent without, glabrous within, long ciliate. *Flower-heads* terminal, 1·3 cm. in diameter, about 14-flowered. *Bracteoles* 5 mm. long, 1 mm. broad at the base, ovate-lanceolate, acuminate, with a long black mucro, membranous long pilose and ciliate. *Sepals* similar to the bracteoles. *Corolla-tube*, 3 mm. long, glabrous; lobes 6 mm. long, 3 to 3·5 mm. broad, obovate, shortly acuminate, obtuse. *Anthers* subsessile, 1·5 mm. long, linear, sagittate at the base. *Ovary* 1 mm. long, globose, pilose; style 2 mm. long, terete, glabrous; stigma minutely bifid. (National Herb. Pretoria, No. 2600.)

---

PLATE 118.—Fig. 1, corolla laid open; 2, bract and bracteole; 3, leaf and calyx; 4, anther; 5, pistil; 6, cross-section of ovary.

F.P.S.A., 1923.

S. GOWER DEL.

# PLATE 119.

*EULOPHIA* ZEYHERI.
*Cape Province, Transvaal, Natal, Basutoland.*

ORCHIDACEAE. *Tribe* VANDEAE.

*EULOPHIA, R. Br.; Benth. et Hook. f. Gen. Plant.*
**Eulophia Zeyheri**, *Hook. f. Bot. Mag. t. 7330; Bolus Ic. Orch. Austr.-Afr.*

This pretty little orchid is quite a common plant in the grass veld during the summer months, and has been extensively gathered by botanical collectors, though strangely enough it is not generally met with in gardens. It has been known to botanists for about sixty years, but under the name *E. bicolor*, until Sir Joseph Hooker in 1893 pointed out that this name had already been assigned to another species in the genus, and published the present name *E. Zeyheri.*

The tubers resemble a string of large beads, and send out leaves and roots from the constrictions between the swollen portions. The plant has been successfully grown in Gloucestershire, England, by the late Mr. H. J. Elwes, and should certainly receive the attention of South African cultivators.

Our illustration was made from specimens collected by Dr. I. B. Pole Evans, C.M.G., at Irene, near Pretoria.

DESCRIPTION:—An acaulescent herb with large underground fleshy tubers 7 cm. long, about 5 cm. in diameter, and thick cylindric roots arising from the junction of the tuber and short stem. *Leaves* three to four to a plant, 19 to 30 cm. long, 1·5 to 3 cm. broad, lanceolate linear, subacuminate, acute, plicate, with the primary nerves prominent beneath, glabrous. *Inflorescence* lateral, racemose, about 26-flowered. *Peduncle* about 30 cm. long, surrounded by brown membranous sheaths 8 to 9 cm. long. *Floral-bracts* 4 cm. long, linear, acuminate, acute. *Pedicels* about 6 mm. long. *Sepals* 2·8 cm. long, 1·1 cm. broad, ovate-lanceolate, shortly acuminate, acute, the upper sepal slightly narrower. *Side petals* 2·6 cm. long, 1 cm. broad, lanceolate, acute. *Lip* 3 cm. long, 1·3 cm. broad, 3-lobed; the middle lobe, obovate, obtuse, sparsely covered with short filaments and produced at the base into 2 keels; side lobes deep purple, 8 mm. long, 9 mm. broad, ovate-oblong, obtuse, unequal sided; spur 5 mm. long, slightly curved, terete, blunt. *Column* 1 cm. long, 3 mm. broad, oblong, convex on the back, deeply concave on the face. *Operculum* ovate; pollinia ovate, attached to a single gland. *Stigma* kidney-shaped. (National Herb. Pretoria, No. 2650.)

---

PLATE 119.—Fig. 1, plant much reduced; 2, bract; 3, median longitudinal section of flower; 4, sepal; 5, side petal; 6, 7, lip; 8, column.

F.P.S.A., 1923.

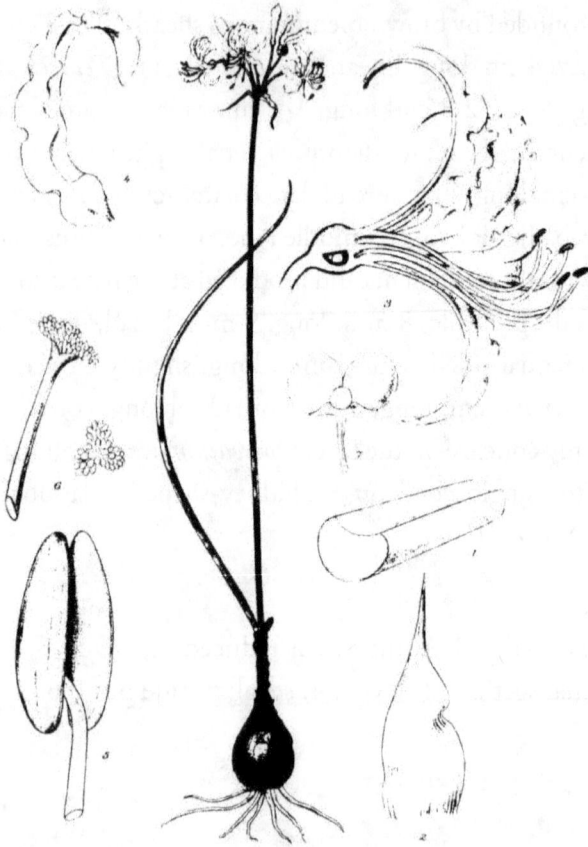

S. GOWER DEL.

# PLATE 120.

*HESSEA REHMANNI.*
*Transvaal.*

AMARYLLIDACEAE. *Tribe* AMARYLLIDEAE.

*HESSEA, Herb.; Benth. et Hook. f. Gen. Plant.*
**Hessea Rehmanni**, *Baker, Hanb. Amaryllid. 22; Fl.*

This species differs from the one we previously figured (*H. Zeyheri*, Plate 43) in not having a short perianth-tube above the ovary. The species here figured is evidently quite common in some localities in the High Veld, growing amongst the grass, but has not been extensively collected. Rehmann first found the plant on which Baker based his description, and it has since been found by Miss Saunders and Mr. E. E. Galpin near Johannesburg. Our illustration was made from specimens collected by Dr. I. B. Pole Evans, C.M.G., at Kaalfontein, between Pretoria and Johannesburg.

Baker in his description mentions that the pedicels are strongly angled, but we suspect that is solely due to drying, as in the fresh material the pedicels are quite terete.

Like many other plants belonging to the *Amaryllidaceae*, the seeds may commence germination before falling from the capsule.

As far as we are aware the species has no common name, and we would suggest "wit sambrieltje" for this little plant.

DESCRIPTION:—*Bulb* 1·8 cm. long, 1·5 cm. in diameter, globose, covered with papery tunics and produced into a neck about 1 to 1·5 cm. long. *Leaves* usually one, more rarely two, 9 cm. long, filiform, quite terete or with a shallow channel, glabrous. *Peduncle* 15 cm. long, terete, glabrous. *Inflorescence* a centripetal umbel of about nine flowers. *Spathe-valves* 2 mm. long, ovate, acute. *Pedicels* 8 mm. long, terete, glabrous. *Perianth-segments* 8 mm. long, 1·5 mm. broad, linear, much crisped, with 3 segments minutely and bluntly apiculate and with papillae at the apex. *Filaments* attached to base of perianth-segments, 5 mm. long, terete; anthers 1 mm. long, orbicular, basifixed. *Ovary* 2·5 mm. in diameter, globose, glabrous with a single ovule in each cell; style 7 mm. long, terete; stigmas 3, papillose. (National Herb. Pretoria, No. 2713.)

PLATE 120.—Fig. 1, section of part of leaf showing shallow channel; 2, involucral bract; 3, median longitudinal section of flower; 4, perianth segment; 5, anther; 6, style and stigmas; 7, fruit.

F.P.S.A., 1923.

# INDEX TO VOLUME III